Extremists for Love

Extremists for Love

A Theological Introduction to the Struggle for Racial Justice in America

J. T. YOUNG

WIPF & STOCK · Eugene, Oregon

EXTREMISTS FOR LOVE
A Theological Introduction to the Struggle for Racial Justice in America

Copyright © 2024 J. T. Young. All rights reserved. Except for brief quotations in critical publications or reviews, no part of this book may be reproduced in any manner without prior written permission from the publisher. Write: Permissions, Wipf and Stock Publishers, 199 W. 8th Ave., Suite 3, Eugene, OR 97401.

Wipf & Stock
An Imprint of Wipf and Stock Publishers
199 W. 8th Ave., Suite 3
Eugene, OR 97401

www.wipfandstock.com

PAPERBACK ISBN: 978-1-6667-7678-2
HARDCOVER ISBN: 978-1-6667-7679-9
EBOOK ISBN: 978-1-6667-7680-5

Scripture quotations are from New Revised Standard Version Bible, copyright © 1989 National Council of the Churches of Christ in the United States of America. Used by permission. All rights reserved worldwide.

07/29/24

For Boston, Oakley, and Kaldi—
In the hope that you'll all become extremists for love
in your own ways.

We cannot segregate God's word from the historical reality in which it is proclaimed. It would not then be God's word.... It would be a pious book, a Bible that is just a book in our library. It becomes God's word because it vivifies, enlightens, contrasts, repudiates, praises what is going on today in this society.

—Oscar Romero

Contents

How to Use This Book		ix
Preface		xiii
Acknowledgments		xvii
1	Martin Luther King Jr.	1
2	James Cone	7
3	Angela Davis	12
4	Nat Turner	18
5	Cornel West	24
6	James Baldwin	30
7	Sojourner Truth	37
8	John Brown	44
9	The Black Panther Party	50
10	Kendrick Lamar	57
11	Harriet Tubman	63
12	Ella Baker	69
13	Malcolm X	75
14	William J. Barber II	83
15	Coretta Scott King	89
16	Fannie Lou Hamer	95
17	Ida B. Wells-Barnett	101
18	Colin Kaepernick	108

Contents

19	Michelle Alexander	113
20	The Black Lives Matter Movement	119
Epilogue		125
Bibliography		127

How to Use This Book

IT'S NO SECRET THAT every book isn't going to appeal to every audience. The current work is no different. It's openly geared toward specific audiences, particularly two: first and foremost, this book is meant for Christians who believe in a God of liberation. American Christianity is easily eclipsed by the popular history of evangelicalism and its emphasis on the salvation of the immaterial soul. While belief in the salvation of an immaterial soul isn't inherently harmful, a theology which focuses *almost exclusively* on an immaterial soul has the potential to lend itself to violence against material bodies.

I once attended a protest in support of Leonard "Raheem" Taylor—a man sentenced to death (and ultimately executed) for the killing of his girlfriend and her children despite evidence that he was out of the state at the time of the murder. A woman who wandered past the demonstration and read our signs started talking to us about what a tragedy it would be if the execution wasn't halted. "But" she said, "if he's put his trust in the Lord, he has nothing to worry about. If our souls are with God, then it doesn't matter what happens to our bodies."

It's this very brand of theology that slavers and white supremacists long used to oppress and dominate people of color. By pushing a vehement theology that disregards bodies and elevates souls, the destruction of material life is easily sanctioned, or even encouraged. When we talk about liberation, we can't only talk about the liberation of the soul; we must also talk about the liberation of the body.

How to Use This Book

This book is for those Christians who believe in a God who has a vested interest in the liberation of these oppressed bodies. It can be used as a devotional for private reflection or merely as a resource to deepen both your understanding of historical racial justice leaders and personal piety as it relates to social justice issues in the world. Each chapter is equipped with reflection prompts at the end, which can be used to either help you think critically about the issues at hand or serve as good points-of-departure for journaling and friendly discussion, as well as a list of further resources you can use to dig deeper into that respective chapter's subject.

Second, this book is meant for pastors and ministry professionals. Many religious leaders, myself included, know the frustration of wanting to lead in the work of justice, educate about racism, and spark important conversations within their congregation, but not knowing how or where to start. Without an approachable vehicle with which to broach these topics within a parish where they may have never previously been discussed, the odds of the discussion getting initiated are low at best.

This text is designed to be a resource to help narrow the gap so many leaders exist in, between the conviction to be a social justice leader in the community and the actual opportunity to be one. This text can easily be utilized as a small-group study to help introduce people to the history of the struggle for racial justice, as well as broaden people's understanding of popular figures within that history. It could also be employed as a social media campaign, with excerpts and reflection questions posted daily for a set period of time. There are many possibilities of how this work can be used to fit different needs and contexts.

But this is a book geared toward religious leaders for another reason, as well. The work of ministry, regardless of context, is often governed by weekly meeting agendas, denominational paperwork, funerals, sermon writing, and the challenge of maintaining the ever-present bottom line. In the grind of day-to-day ministry, it can be easy to lose sight of the scandalous nature of the gospel. This story promises good news to the poor, release to the captive, healing for the sick, inclusion for the outcast, and hope for the hopeless.

This book is for the pastor or ministry leader who needs to be reminded of that story. A professor I had in seminary once said that the church's greatest and most valuable asset is a healthy pastor. But discouragement and apathy will quickly set in if we become convinced that the sum of the ministerial calling is nothing more than answering emails and making sure the bulletins are printed on time. For the leader struggling with spiritual acedia—what the ancient monk Evagrius of Pontus called the "noonday devil"[1]—this book can help refresh the purpose of our calling, reminding us that the ministry of the church and the first fruits of the gospel don't belong to us, but to "the least of these."[2]

---

1. Nault, *Noonday Devil*, 28.
2. Matt 25:45.

Preface

SOMETIME IN EARLY 2016, shortly after my son was born the previous fall, I was walking through Labyrinth Books—my favorite bookstore in Princeton, New Jersey. It was a weekend and Nassau Street was busier than usual, bustling with other students and young families taking advantage of the sunny day after months of dreary winter. My partner, Aimes, and I, desperate to get out of our small grad-student apartment, decided to take our newborn for a walk downtown.

After wandering through Labyrinth and scanning their impressively extensive sections on religion, philosophy, and politics, we began navigating toward the store's exit. As we were weaving in and out of the people with our bulky jogging stroller, though, the outline of a familiar figure politely passed us going the other direction. Aimes and I looked at each other and then back at the figure, immediately confirming our suspicions. A few feet behind us, carrying a tall, wobbly stack of books in his arms, was Dr. Cornel West—the radical intellectual whose career regularly vacillated between lecturing in Ivy League classrooms and getting arrested at racial justice protests.

I suddenly changed course, veering around a table covered in newly released paperbacks and unashamedly going against the flow of foot traffic. I knew that I might never get another opportunity to meet him, so I wasn't going to miss this one. "Excuse me, Professor West?" I sheepishly introduced myself as a master's student at Princeton Seminary and thanked him for his important

Preface

scholarship (which I had heavily engaged in my college years after the murder of Michael Brown in Ferguson, Missouri).

When Aimes finally caught up with the stroller in tow, I introduced them to one another and gently pulled back the stroller's shade to reveal our newest addition sleeping through the excitement. "This is my son, Boston," I said. "Well, hello Boston!" Dr. West proclaimed. "It's so great to have you in the world! We're trying to make this place a little bit better."

Dr. West's sentiment gives language to my hopes for this little book. I'm under no delusion that the present work will change the world or eradicate the specter of racism. To a large extent, reflective, intellectual labor such as this is complementary at best. It can't replace street protests, public space occupation, community engagement, legal advocacy, or any other form of on-the-ground activism. At the same time, though, until people become educated and enlightened on important social issues, activism can't take place to begin with. So, if this undertaking can help people become even slightly more invested in liberation for the black community, it just might be able to make this world a little bit better.

This project is being birthed in the aftermath of the killing of Tyre Nichols—an unarmed black man beaten to death by six police officers on the streets of Memphis, Tennessee. A young man interested in skateboarding and photography, who was apprehended by police less than a football field away from his house, Tyre is (as of this writing) one of the most recent victims in a seemingly uninterrupted string of black, unarmed, police-related deaths held up in the national spotlight: Trayvon Martin, Michael Brown, Tamir Rice, Eric Garner, Philando Castile, Elijah McClain, Breonna Taylor, George Floyd, Daunte Wright, Tyre Nichols.

This list is by no means exhaustive (and doesn't do justice to the long list of other black women and LGBTQ+ people killed by police, despite rarely making a blip on the media radar). There were others killed before and after them; these are merely *some* of the ones that made it into national headlines. And yet, even though this list is far from complete, it's long enough and disorienting enough to present us with a warped concept of time. With

Preface

so many events of police brutality saturating our cultural dialogue, it's easy for them to amalgamate and become confused, blending into a single, consistent act of violence. We know these individuals' names and that they were killed; we might even remember the circumstances and locations of their killings, but often can't recall the order, months, or even years of most of them. This kind of amnesia should be interpreted as a warning. If we become intellectually complacent in our recognition of patterns of racism, then the relentless onslaught of systemic racial oppression in America—made plain by police murder—runs the risk of becoming further and further normalized.

Much of our culture and society want people to dismiss their direct observations of the world around them. The narrative of "bad apples" and "not all cops" is nothing more than an effort to pull wool over our eyes; to make us forget. My hope is that this book will help us remember—the names, the patterns, the systems, and our Christian responsibility to never be neutral regarding injustice.

Jesus takes sides. So should we.

Acknowledgments

IN A 1946 ESSAY, outlining his own journey toward becoming a writer, George Orwell made a stark observation: "Writing a book is a horrible, exhausting struggle, like a long bout of some painful illness. One would never undertake such a thing if one were not driven on by some demon whom one can neither resist or understand."[1] Over the last year of working on this project, I've found *almost* all of this sentiment to be true. The one place I disagree, though, is the idea that writing a book is driven by a demon one cannot understand.

I know exactly why I was compelled to write this book. It is, in a way, still far too small and insignificant, an act of penance; an offering of contrition for all the years spent unable or unwilling to understand the systemic oppression black and brown communities have perpetually endured. This journey of anti-racism is one which never ends. No matter how long we travel, the destination will remain forever in the distance. I hope I am much further ahead now than I was a decade ago when I took the first step, but openly acknowledge that I have much further to go. It, like writing a book, is also an "exhausting struggle." These are both journeys which no person can undertake without the love and support of friends, many of whom I have to thank here.

Many of my colleagues in ministry—both those situated in the parish and in the academy—read drafts, offered feedback, and provided encouragement along the way, undoubtedly making this work better than it would have been otherwise. I extend appreciation to

1. Orwell, *Why I Write*, 10.

Acknowledgments

Kyle Baldwin, Dr. Luke Bobo, Rev. Ali Fields, Rev. Dr. Kate Hanch, Dr. Christopher Hunt, Rev. Danny Lybarger, Dr. W. Travis McMaken, S. G. Seymour, Jacobi Spresser, and Dr. Christian Collins Winn.

Finally, my most abundant gratitude is due to my family. During the course of writing this book, there were many times when they lost me to my desk; many movie nights, dinners, and activities were put on the back burner in order to support me in this work. The burden of my absence fell largely on my partner, Aimes, who in addition to picking up my slack at home, carried out invaluable research assistance, graciously read through the entirety of the manuscript and offered continuous comment and reassurance. Thank you for always throwing light into my darkest corners, even when I don't know I need it.

And to my kids, Boston, Oakley, and Kaldi: you three have been like little lighthouses in the midst of a tempestuous sea, always reminding me that there is still light in the darkness. Thank you for always being my personal bearers of hope. This book is for you.

1

Martin Luther King Jr.

But the judgment of God is upon the church as never before. If today's church does not recapture the sacrificial spirit of the early church, it will lose its authentic ring, forfeit the loyalty of millions, and be dismissed as an irrelevant social club with no meaning for the twentieth century. Every day I meet young people whose disappointment with the church has turned into outright disgust.[1]

—Martin Luther King Jr. (1929–1968)

With what shall I come before the LORD, and bow myself before God on high? Shall I come before him with burnt offerings, with calves a year old? Will the LORD be pleased with thousands of rams, with ten thousands of rivers of oil? Shall I give my firstborn for my transgression, the fruit of my body for the sin of my soul? He has told you, O mortal, what is good; and what does the LORD require of you but to do justice, and to love kindness, and to walk humbly with your God?

—Micah 6:6–8

---

1. King, "Letter," 300.

Extremists for Love

I grew up in St. Louis, about twenty minutes west of the place Michael Brown was murdered and the subsequent Ferguson Uprising. A university student at the time, I was embarrassingly naïve to the ongoing systemic issues of race in America. I, like many, was effectively taught that the Civil Rights Movement resolved the problem of racism. After all, a black man was president of the United States. How much racism could possibly still be pervading this country?

It wasn't until the following spring that I got my answer. The professor supervising my degree program in religion offered a special topics class called "Race, Rights, and Religion after Ferguson." It was during this course that the scales began to fall from my eyes. Racism wasn't an obsolete concept or relic of history; it was alive and well and thriving.

Though, like most people, I had a generic familiarity with Martin Luther King Jr., it wasn't until this course of study that I actually began to study him on his own terms. Famous for, among many other things, his endorsement of nonviolence, King's philosophy can be easily dismissed by the novice historical observer as nothing more than immoderate sentimentality. This viewpoint is thrown into doubt, however, when we consider the stringent nonresistance training protestors had to undergo in order to be physically and emotionally prepared for remaining stoic in the face of violence.

Much like his philosophy, though, King has often been overly romanticized. Yes, his goal was racial equality and freedom for the black population in America, but he knew the issue of racism didn't develop in a vacuum (a phrase you'll see several times throughout this book). It was a part of a system of thorough inequality that ran through other aspects of the culture, too. King famously derided America's obsession with what he called the "giant triplets"—racism, economic exploitation, and militarism.[2]

For King, these three were inevitably tethered to one another. Those subject to oppression due to race, poverty, and war were *all* in need of equality and freedom. Though not widely taught or

2. King, "Three Evils of Society."

publicized when discussing King's legacy, he passionately advocated for conditions and policies that would directly counter these three evils: universal basic income for all people, a high marginal tax rate for the rich, $10 million income cap, and universal government-funded healthcare systems.

And if anyone should be concerned about these issues, it should be the church. King, ever a product of Christianity both through his family history and ministerial training, both held the church to a high standard and was consistently disappointed with its commitments. Rather than fighting against the injustice of racism, many churches chose to uphold the status quo, thus putting them out of step with the modern needs of the people Jesus directly served on earth: the poor, oppressed, and downtrodden.

In 1960, King said, "any religion that professes to be concerned about the souls of men and is not concerned about the slums that damn them, the economic conditions that strangle them and the social conditions that cripple them is a spiritually moribund religion awaiting burial."[3] Here, we see a correlation with King's "giant triplets." According to King, if the church is not at least equally as concerned with the worldly, concrete conditions of humanity as it is the metaphysical, immaterial conditions of the soul, then it is an institution primed to die.

King's frustration with the church is similar to that expressed by Micah in the Old Testament concerning the behavior of Israel: ritual, sacrifice, and offerings are meaningless if they don't find an outward, social expression. These are meant to be symbols that remind us of God's liberative action in the world—the action that freed the Israelites from slavery in Egypt and freed the peasant Jesus from the oppression of death—in order that we will go out into the world and liberate others. However, when we use these practices as attempts to gatekeep access to God's favor, justice, and deliverance, they cease to be divine customs and become oppressive constraints.

King envisioned what he called the "Beloved Community"— a community free from hate, discrimination, oppression, poverty,

---

3. King, "Pilgrimage to Nonviolence," 38.

need, and fear. This is the community he appeals to in his famous "I Have a Dream" speech when he calls forth the image of a day when black children and white children can play together, the descendants of slaves and slave-owners can sit together, and all will have equity and freedom. This "Beloved Community," for King, is what the church needs to ever be striving towards, lest it resist and remain static too long and become obsolete.

REFLECT

1. King mentions the "judgment of God" being on the church as never before. Reflect on the church of the twenty-first century: has anything changed? What aspects of its identity might be under God's judgment today?
2. Read again the passage from Micah at the beginning of the chapter. The three qualities it endorses in the last verse are justice, kindness, and humility. In what ways are you or your religious community living into these? In what ways can you or your religious community live into them better?
3. Think about King's "giant triplets": racism, economic exploitation, and militarism. Do you think these are still problems we're facing in twenty-first-century America? Why or why not? What might be the reasons someone believes the opposite from you?
4. The church has long tried to gatekeep the Bible, religious practices, and community inclusion from specific groups of people based on their race, nationality, country of origin, sexual identity and orientation, etc. Think critically about your religious community; can you identify any gatekeeping practices? If you do, how might you go about changing them and making the community more inclusive?
5. King was heavily concerned about a religion that only cared about the salvation of souls and not the material conditions of the world. As you audit your own faith and faith community,

do you find a balance of concern for both bodies and souls? Are there ways you or your faith community can incorporate concern for the poor and oppressed more heavily into the vision and practice of ministry?

KEEP READING

Martin Luther King Jr.

Stride toward Freedom: The Montgomery Story. New York: Harper, 1958.
A Testament of Hope: The Essential Writings and Speeches of Martin Luther King, Jr. Edited by James M. Washington. New York: Harper Collins, 1991.
Where Do We Go from Here: Chaos or Community? Boston: Beacon Press, 1968.
Why We Can't Wait. Boston: Beacon Press, 1968.

Peter J. Albert and Ronald Hoffman

We Shall Overcome: Martin Luther King, Jr. and the Black Freedom Struggle. New York: Da Capo, 1993.

James Cone

Martin and Malcolm and America: A Dream or a Nightmare. Maryknoll, NY: Orbis, 2012.

Noel Leo Erskine

King among the Theologians. Cleveland: Pilgrim, 1994.

David J. Garrow

Bearing the Cross: Martin Luther King, Jr., and the Southern Christian Leadership Conference. New York: Vintage Books, 1988.

Luther D. Ivory

Toward a Theology of Radical Involvement: The Theological Legacy of Martin Luther King, Jr. Nashville: Abingdon, 1997.

Thomas F. Jackson

From Civil Rights to Human Rights: Martin Luther King, Jr., and the Struggle for Economic Justice. Philadelphia: University of Pennsylvania Press, 2007.

Extremists for Love

Richard Lischer
The Preacher King: Martin Luther King, Jr., and the Word That Moved America. New York: Oxford University Press, 1995.

Gerald McKnight
The Last Crusade: Martin Luther King, Jr., the FBI, and the Poor People's Campaign. Boulder, CO: Westview, 1998.

2

James Cone

The gospel is the proclamation of God's liberation as revealed in the event of Jesus and the outpouring of the Holy Spirit. It is not possible to receive the good news of freedom and keep it to ourselves; it must be told to the whole world... To preach the gospel today means confronting the world with the reality of Christian freedom. It means telling blacks that their slavery has come to an end, and telling whites to let go of the chains.[1]

—James Cone (1938–2018)

Go therefore and make disciples of all nations, baptizing them in the name of the Father and of the Son and of the Holy Spirit, and teaching them to obey everything that I have commanded you. And remember, I am with you always, to the end of the age.

—Matthew 28:19–20

Every person of faith has an aspect of their faith or identity which helps determine the way everything else is understood. This is called our "point of departure." This "point" can be thought of

---

1. Cone, *Black Theology of Liberation*, 138–39.

as the center of one's faith, the measuring stick by which all of our other beliefs and commitments are compared, the place where our faith begins and ends. Our understanding of different issues and ideas all flow from this center and are informed by it. For some, this point is a concept of salvation from eternal torment. For others, it might be the figure of Jesus and his sacrifice on the cross. Whatever that point of departure is, it's the first line of defense when we consider how to make sense of the world around us and God's presence in it.

For James Cone, though, that point of departure isn't salvation or the figure of Jesus or any of the other options American Christians have traditionally opted for; no, his point of departure was *black oppression*. In his groundbreaking book *A Black Theology of Liberation*, Cone expressed his frustration with how the white church has long neglected the plight of black people in the United States: "No white theologian has ever taken the oppression of blacks as a point of departure for analyzing God's activity in contemporary America."[2] So, seeing the gap in the system left by predominantly white academics, Cone steps in and does what no one else to that point had done.

Cone began his career in earnest at the breaking point of the struggle for racial equality in the United States. He published his first book, *Black Theology and Black Power*,[3] in 1969 in the aftermath of Jim Crow, the murder of Dr. Martin Luther King Jr., and the emergence of black revolutionary groups like the Black Panther Party (which we'll talk about later). While dealing with the social turmoil of his time, Cone set out to think theologically about the oppression of black Americans and the role that the church and theology have played in that oppression.

A polarizing figure in American Christianity, Cone didn't hesitate to utilize racial language in his theology: "Black theology proclaims God's blackness . . . Knowing God means being on the side of the oppressed, becoming *one* with them, and participating

---

2. Cone, *Black Theology of Liberation*, 9.
3. Cone, *Black Theology and Black Power*.

in the goal of liberation. *We must become black with God!*⁴ For many, the idea of "God's blackness" is difficult to comprehend. How can God have a race? But in reality, that's not really what Cone is trying to get at.

Instead of trying to assign God a literal, genetic race, this idea of blackness for Cone is a symbol "which describes what oppression means in America."⁵ So saying that God is black is Cone's way of saying that God identifies with and understands the suffering and oppression of black people. And if we desire to engage in this work of liberation as well, then we also must "become black"; we must also seek to identify and understand the suffering and oppression of black people. It's the people willing to take on this burden who, for Cone, make up the church.

At this time, the church in America was heavily divided by race, both literally and figuratively, and so Cone had an important question to answer: if two Christian communities have wildly different ideas about the oppressed black community, then which one is the true, authentic church? In other words, how do we differentiate theologically between churches who endorse white supremacy and churches who endorse black liberation?

Cone solves this problem of where to find the authentic church by changing the point of departure altogether. Traditionally, the church was understood as the gathering together of believers who both (1) preached the Bible, and (2) celebrated the sacraments. But if two churches with competing ethical ideas of race are both doing these things, then we need a new standard by which we can measure them, and Cone provides that: "Participation in the historical liberation spearheaded by God is the defining characteristic of the church."⁶

This defining characteristic pervades Cone's idea of what the church should be and what it should be doing. For Cone, a gathering of people coming together to read the Bible and partake in the sacraments isn't the true church at all insofar as it finds its identity

---

4. Cone, *Black Theology of Liberation*, 69, emphasis original.
5. Cone, *Black Theology of Liberation*, 8.
6. Cone, *Black Theology of Liberation*, 138.

in those things. Rather, the true church is a gathering of people coming together to partake in this "historical liberation" that God is leading. Through this new definition, Cone reinterprets the "great commission" we find in Matt 28 and provides a new, timely definition not wrapped up in convincing people to accept a set of theological ideas, but in confronting oppressive powers in the world.

In Cone's quote at the top of the chapter, he says that "to preach the gospel today means confronting the world with the reality of Christian freedom. It means telling blacks that their slavery has come to an end, and telling whites to let go of the chains." So, one of the most important tasks for us (particularly white) Christians today is to take a step back from our own faith and ego and fragility and ask in what ways we might be still holding the chains of oppression, and what we need to do to let go of them. Liberation work is God's work. And if God is engaged in the battle of liberation, then we should be as well.

REFLECT

1. At the top of this chapter, we talked about what it means to have a "point of departure" for our particular faith journey. What would you say your personal point of departure is? What about your church or faith community? Is it something you think is in line with the liberation of oppressed people, like Cone talks about, or is it something you need to examine anew?

2. Cone's project aimed to address disparities between the popular theologies of the day and the lived, embodied experiences of black oppression in twentieth-century America. Do you still see these disparities in our current church? Why or why not?

3. Think about Cone's idea of "becoming black." In light of the recent social unrest stemming from the murder of unarmed black people by police, what do you think this means for

the church in the twenty-first century? How can and should the church "become black" today in our specific historical context?

4. What do you think about the way Cone renegotiates the "litmus test" for what is and isn't a legitimate Christian community? Do you think churches can preach the Bible and celebrate the sacraments without being authentic expressions of the body of Christ?

5. As a follow-up to question 4, do you think *your* church community would pass Cone's test? Why or why not? If not, how can you begin to shift your ministry such that it begins thinking critically about the plight of the oppressed and contributing to the efforts of liberation?

KEEP READING

James Cone

Black Theology: A Documentary History (Volume One) 1966–1979. Maryknoll, NY: Orbis, 1993.
Black Theology and Black Power. New York: Seabury, 1969.
A Black Theology of Liberation. Maryknoll, NY: Orbis, 2015.
The Cross and the Lynching Tree. Maryknoll, NY: Orbis, 2013.
God of the Oppressed. Maryknoll, NY: Orbis, 1997.
Said I Wasn't Gonna Tell Nobody: The Making of a Black Theologian. Maryknoll, NY: Orbis, 2018.

Noel Leo Erskine

Black Theology and Black Faith. Grand Rapids: Eerdmans, 2023.

3

Angela Davis

We must strive to "lift as we climb." In other words, we must climb in such a way as to guarantee that all of our sisters, regardless of social class, and indeed all of our brothers, climb with us. This must be the essential dynamic of our quest for power—a principle that must not only determine our struggles as Afro-American women, but also govern all authentic struggles of dispossessed people.[1]

—Angela Davis (1944–)

Listen, my beloved brothers and sisters. Has not God chosen the poor in the world to be rich in faith and to be heirs of the kingdom that he has promised to those who love him? But you have dishonored the poor. Is it not the rich who oppress you? Is it not they who drag you into court?

—James 2:5–6

In 1970, Jonathon Jackson smuggled weapons into a Marin County, California, courthouse and interrupted an unfolding trial. In an attempt at leveraging a deal to free his brother from prison,

---

1. Davis, *Women, Culture, and Politics*, 5.

Jackson and several accomplices took hostages, including the judge and members of the jury. The ensuing situation ultimately left four dead, including the court's judge and Jackson himself. The guns used in the takeover, however, weren't registered to Jackson or any of the other accomplices for that matter. Instead, they were registered to a recently terminated UCLA professor who was in New York City at the time of the shooting. Thus, given this professor's relationship to the crime's weapons, California Governor Ronald Reagan put out a warrant for the arrest of one Angela Yvonne Davis.

Davis was captured in New York some two months later and extradited back to California where she was held in solitary confinement for over a year until her trial started in 1972.[2] Davis was ultimately acquitted of all charges (by an all-white jury of her "peers," no less) after no connection could be established between her and the actual plot of the courtroom takeover. The fact that her guns turned up at the scene of the crime was immaterial after it was clear she wasn't in on the scheme. But considering her politically revolutionary activity in the months and years leading up to the events at the Marin County courthouse, the state finding a way to put Davis behind bars wasn't necessarily a surprise.

After all, the concept of "revolution" often carries a bit of a negative connotation, doesn't it? At least when we think about it in political terms, it's often associated with violence, destruction, and death. And though those things might be unfortunate—albeit inevitable—by-products of a political revolution, they're certainly not the purpose or goal, and Davis knew that better than anyone.

"The Face of Revolution."[3] That is the title Lilia Luciano, a journalist for *CBS News*, bestowed on Davis in her introduction to their 2022 interview. And it's a title which, in my humble opinion, Davis has earned. Even if you're unfamiliar with her name, you'd likely still recognize her iconic Afro and raised fist; symbols of an era defined by radical black resistance to oppression and prejudice.

Born into a segregated Birmingham, Alabama, Davis was baptized in that reality of racial oppression at an early age. In a

---

2. For a robust overview of Davis's trial, see Aptheker, *Dawn Breaks*.
3. Davis, "Continuing to Fight."

2013 interview, she recalled that her parents were active in social and political organizing before she was born, and that one of her earliest memories of engaging in this kind of work was attending an interracial discussion group at her church in 1955.[4] Her "claim to fame," however, doesn't have to do with her upbringing as much as her political involvement in the late 1960s and early 1970s.

While completing her PhD and teaching at the University of California, Los Angeles, Davis came under fire (figuratively and literally) for her membership in the Communist Party, USA, a decision made out of acknowledgment that "to win, we had to fight and the fight that would win was the one collectively waged by the masses of our people and working people in general."[5] Davis, like the others we've talked about thus far, was very much an "intersectional" thinker. That isn't a term we've used yet, but it can be applied to Davis, Cone, King, and probably most (if not all) the figures we'll talk about in this book. By "intersectional," I mean that she understands that modes of injustice and oppression develop alongside and thrive off one another. Inequality based on race, gender, sexuality, health, socioeconomic status, and others do not exist independently; they're interconnected in a complex web of social and political realities.

We can see this kind of intersectional thinking in the brief quotation at the top of the chapter. This quote comes from a lecture Davis gave to the National Women's Studies Association in 1987 in which she was referencing the feminist movement and how it has often ignored the challenges uniquely faced by black women. For Davis, there's something unique to be said about the way injustice based on race and gender compound to afflict black women in different, and often harsher, ways than white women or men of any race. Thus, if the sufferings of black women can be addressed in the struggle for civil rights, then the sufferings of other oppressed women (and men, as she points out) will *also* be addressed.

Likewise, in the same context, she uses the language of "social class," thus gesturing toward how economic discrimination

4. Davis and Platt, "Interview," 38.
5. Davis, *Angela Davis*, 187.

intersects with race and gender as well. In the same way race and gender create a kind of compounded oppression for black women, so poverty adds *another* layer of injustice for black women who might inherit poverty from their families or find themselves in poverty some other way, but are unable to escape it due to discriminatory practices of employment, housing, law enforcement, etc.

This economic component brings to mind the passage quoted above from the book of James. In it, the author addresses a practice in the early Christian communities of favoring the rich and privileged over the poor and dispossessed, asking rhetorically, "Has God not chosen the poor . . . to be heirs of the kingdom?" Much like Davis, the author of James thinks intersectionally; elsewhere in the same epistle, the issues of vulnerable women and children, hunger, and housing insecurity are addressed, telling the rich that they should "weep and wail for the miseries that are coming."[6]

For both Davis and the book of James, hope isn't something necessarily supernatural or otherworldly. Instead, it's the concrete potential for a better world that needs to be worked out in *this life*. And while we can read James and be inspired by the biblical call for justice and equality, a figure the likes of Davis can help us interpret what that justice and equality might need to look like in twenty-first-century America. Those of us Christians who are convicted to carry out the work of social justice *need* the Bible, but, in a very real way, we also *need* Davis to help teach us what it should mean today.

REFLECT

1. Think about this idea of "intersectionality." What issues in our contemporary American context do you see intersecting with one another, and how?
   - Activity: Select one specific issue that is of particular importance to you or your group and write it either in the middle of a piece of paper or a dry-erase board.

---

6. Jas 5:1.

From there, generate a bubble map by listing out other issues that intersect with it and talk about the specific ways those issues intersect with the main one.

2. Davis talks about how sometimes well-meaning social movements (like feminism) often tend to neglect the issues of people not a part of the majority race, class, etc. Can you think of any communities or identities which are still being ostracized and ignored by social movements *today*?

3. In the late 1960s and early 1970s, Davis worked closely with the Black Panther Party (which we'll talk about later in chapter 9)—a radical organization devoted to black liberation. The idea of organizing around a commonly held conviction is important in the work for social justice, regardless of the particular issue in question. Thinking specifically about racial justice, what are some ways you can join in the work of a group or organization already dedicated to this work, or how do you think you and your community (religious or otherwise) can come together to establish that kind of justice-oriented group?

4. According to the 2021 census, there are nearly forty million people living in poverty in America[7] while existing alongside some of the wealthiest ultrarich billionaires in history. In light of the message we find in the book of James, how should we as Christians understand this issue of wealth inequality? How should it affect the policies and legislation we may or may not advocate for?

5. In the last several decades of her career, Davis has taken up the cause of racial justice and prisons. We'll talk more about the issue of prisons in chapter 19 when we learn about the work of Michelle Alexander, but, for now, take a moment and consider how the above-mentioned issues of race, gender, and class might intersect with the issue of incarceration in America.

---

7. Burns et al., "Poverty."

KEEP READING

Angela Davis

Abolition Democracy: Beyond Prison, Torture, and Empire. New York: Seven Stories, 2005.
Angela Davis: An Autobiography. New York: International, 1988.
Are Prisons Obsolete? New York: Seven Stories, 2003.
Freedom Is a Constant Struggle: Ferguson, Palestine, and the Foundations of a Movement. Chicago: Haymarket, 2016.
Women, Culture, and Politics. New York: Vintage Books, 1989.
Women, Race, and Class. New York: Vintage Books, 1983.

Angela Davis; Gina Dent; Erica Meiners; Beth Richie

Abolition. Feminism. Now. Chicago: Haymarket, 2022.

Bettina Aptheker

The Morning Breaks: The Trial of Angela Davis. Ithaca, NY: Cornell University Press, 1999.

4

Nat Turner

I heard a loud noise in the heavens, and the Spirit instantly appeared to me and said the Serpent was loosened, and Christ had laid down the yoke he had borne for the sins of men, and that I should take it on and fight against the Serpent, for the time was fast approaching when the first should be last and the last should be first.[1]

—Nat Turner (1800–1831)

I came to bring fire to the earth, and how I wish it were already kindled I have a baptism with which to be baptized, and what stress I am under until it is completed! Do you think that I have come to bring peace to the earth? No, I tell you, but rather division!

—Luke 12:49–51

When our second kiddo was on the way, we found ourselves in the hospital one morning because Aimes started going into early labor around the twentieth week of pregnancy—something any parent will tell you is quite terrifying. We ended up being there for several days as we struggled to get the contractions under

---

1. Turner, *Confessions of Nat Turner*, 19.

control, and during one of those days when Aimes was sleeping and I was working on my computer, my sister sent me a trailer to a new movie that had recently come out. I clicked on the link, not thinking much of it, only to find myself in a puddle of tears two minutes later.

The story followed a young slave in the Antebellum South as he navigated the hostility of oppression, the survival of his family, and the conviction to rebel; a conviction born not out of a mere thirst for revenge or bloodlust but rather a deep, uncompromising piety. The trailer was for the 2016 film *The Birth of a Nation* about the young Nat Turner and the rebellion he cultivated among the slaves in Southampton, Virginia, in 1831. Canonized by some as a prophet and vilified by others as a terrorist, Turner would go on to become near-legendary as (paradoxically) "the most famous, least-known person in American history."[2]

Turner was born on October 2, 1800, to an enslaved family under the ownership of Benjamin Turner. Unlike many enslaved blacks at the time, though, Turner knew how to read and write, showcasing a sharp mind even from childhood. Thomas R. Gray (the man who recorded Turner's testimony in the aftermath of his revolt) assessed Turner as having a "natural intelligence and quickness of apprehension . . . unsurpassed by few men I have ever seen."[3] From a young age, Turner used his intelligence and reading ability to dive deeply into the Bible. He spoke of his younger self and his inclination toward religious zeal, saying, "to a mind like mine, restless, inquisitive and observant of every thing [sic] that was passing, it is easy to suppose that religion was the subject to which it would be directed."[4] And as he grew in wisdom and stature, Turner developed into an effective communicator. A Richmond, Virginia, newspaper reported in the days following the rebellion that, prior to, Turner was "permitted to go about preaching in the country."[5] Assuming these religious gatherings are where

---

2. Greenberg, "Name, Face, Body," 3.
3. Turner, *Confessions of Nat Turner*, 26.
4. Turner, *Confessions of Nat Turner*, 16.
5. French, *Rebellious Slave*, 2.

plans were laid for the uprising, there was a crackdown on unsupervised slave gatherings following the events of 1831, regardless of whether or not they were supposed to be religiously oriented.

But how did Turner arrive at such a religious conviction as to believe he was being divinely compelled to organize a violent uprising against slave owners? The answer to that question lies in Turner's distinct theological framework, equally informed by black slave religion, biblical apocalyptic texts, and (perhaps most importantly) his own religious visions and experiences (which he openly attributed to the working of the Holy Spirit). These experiences came in various ways and forms. In his *Confessions*, he references particular visions in 1825—six years before his rebellion—in which he saw "white spirits and black spirits engaged in battle" and claims to have discovered "drops of blood on the corn as if it were dew from heaven." A critical moment in Turner's visions came a few years later, though, in 1828, when he had the vision mentioned in the quote at the top of this chapter in which the Spirit communicated to him about the "Serpent" that had been loosened. It was after this and subsequent experiences that Turner began hatching a plan for rebellion.

Historian and theologian Karl Lampley identifies Turner's theology as "a political black theology of liberation from slavery through revolutionary counterviolence."[6] While each of those components—political, black, liberation, revolution, and counterviolence—play a specific role within Turner's theological framework (and we unfortunately don't have the space to dive deeply into each of them here), it's clear that Turner's actions weren't carried out with the end of inflicting pain, torture, and revenge on his victims. Rather, Turner viewed these instances of "revolutionary counterviolence" as necessary to the struggle for liberation and freedom.

According to Vincent Gordon Harding, there is a tradition which tells us that Turner's final words to his fellow revolutionaries before they carried out their "work of death" were: "Remember, we do not go forth for the sake of blood and carnage; but it is

---

6. Lampley, *Theological Account*, 67.

necessary that, in the commencement of this revolution, all the whites we meet should die, until we have an army strong enough to carry out the war on a Christian basis. Remember that ours is not a war for robbery, nor to satisfy our passions; it is a struggle for freedom."[7] Within a matter of hours, Turner and his comrades were discovered and pursued by a group of white men who proceeded to capture or kill the majority of the group. Turner was able to escape and hide in the wilderness for nearly two months until he was discovered.

For those of us living in a contemporary America so heavily influenced by Martin Luther King Jr.'s philosophy of nonviolence, Nat Turner's rebellion poses an important question to us: is violence *always* incompatible with the Christian faith, or are there times when violent resistance is a necessary component of the Christian faith? And if violence *can* be divinely sanctioned, then how are we to determine the right place, time, and manner with which to engage in it? Should that determination be made in a once-and-for-all fashion or constantly revisited by individual communities of people experiencing enslavement, persecution, and dehumanization?

These questions—and the distinct question of whether or not people should pass judgment on the ways oppressed communities engage in the struggle for freedom in the first place—are divisive. And it calls to mind Jesus' quote above: "Do you think that I have come to bring peace to the earth? No, I tell you, but rather division!" Turner certainly believed this in a very literal way; a lack of peace for slaveholding whites was necessary to the freedom of the enslaved. But even for modern social justice movements that overwhelmingly engage in nonviolent protests, this concept still holds. There's a reason that many of us who have taken to the streets in recent years to protest the murder of unarmed black people at the hands of the police chant "NO JUSTICE! NO PEACE!" A lack of social, economic, and political peace for oppressive institutions, and the people who enable them, is necessary for change. And, at least according to our passage above, to insist that Jesus would

---

7. Harding, "God's Avenging Scourge," 27.

be neutral or antagonistic to such movements may very well be a misinterpretation of who he was and how he himself understood his ministry on earth.

REFLECT

1. The key idea that defines Turner and his rebellion is this idea of divinely sanctioned violence. Take a few moments and consider the questions asked in the body of the chapter regarding this idea:

    - Is violence *always* incompatible with the Christian faith, or are there times when violence is a necessary component of the Christian faith?

    - If violence *can* be divinely sanctioned, then how are we to determine the right place, time, and manner with which to engage in it?

    - Should that determination be made in a once-and-for-all fashion or constantly revisited by individual communities of people experiencing enslavement, persecution, and dehumanization?

2. There are times in the Gospels when Jesus appears to be very pacifistic, or believing that violence can't be justified, and there are other times when the opposite seems to be true (e.g., Luke 6:29 and Luke 12:49–51). Is it possible to reconcile those two seemingly contradictory convictions? If so, how? If not, how should we accommodate both in our own faiths?

3. Toward the beginning of the chapter, there's a reference to how some revere Turner a prophet, while others vilify him as a terrorist. At this moment, after reading the brief chapter about Turner and his rebellion, where on that spectrum do you find yourself falling? Why? Do you feel like your thoughts might shift one way or the other at any point?

KEEP READING

Nat Turner

The Confessions of Nat Turner, the Leader of the Late Insurrection in Southampton, Va. Edited by Thomas R. Gray. Chapel Hill, NC: DocSouth, 2011.

Scot French

The Rebellious Slave: Nat Turner in American Memory. New York: Houghton Mifflin, 2004.

Kenneth S. Greenberg

"Name, Face, Body." *Nat Turner: A Slave Rebellion in History and Memory.* Edited by Kenneth S. Greenberg. New York: Oxford University Press, 2003.

Vincent Gordon Harding

"God's Avenging Scourge: Nat Turner's Rebellion, the Bloodiest in Slave History, Was Driven by His Prophetic Visions." *Christian History*, 1999, 28–31.

Vanessa M. Holden

Surviving Southampton: African American Women and Resistance in Nat Turner's Community. Champaign: University of Illinois Press, 2021.

Karl W. Lampley

A Theological Account of Nat Turner: Christianity, Violence, and Theology. New York: Palgrave Macmillan, 2013.

Stephen B. Oates

The Fires of Jubilee: Nat Turner's Fierce Rebellion. New York: Harper Perennial, 2016.

5

Cornel West

The three dogmas that are leading in the imperial devouring in America—free-market fundamentalism, aggressive militarism, and escalating authoritarianism—are often justified by the religious rhetoric of . . . Christian fundamentalism. And perhaps most ironically—and sadly—fundamentalism is subverting the most profound, seminal teachings of Christianity, those being that we should live with humility, love our neighbors, and do unto others as we would have them do unto us.[1]

—Cornel West (1953–)

When the Pharisees heard that he had silenced the Sadducees, they gathered together, and one of them, a lawyer, asked him a question to test him. "Teacher, which commandment in the law is the greatest?" He said to him, "'You shall love the Lord your God with all your heart, and with all your soul, and with all your mind.' This is the greatest and first commandment. And a second is like it: 'You shall love your neighbor as yourself.' On these two commandments hang all the law and the prophets."

—Matthew 22:34–40

---

1. West, *Democracy Matters*, 146.

Cornel West

Though we're only just now getting to take an extended look at Cornel West and his work, you might remember that he's already been mentioned. I spoke in the preface about the brief-yet-influential interaction I had with West as a grad student at Princeton Seminary. At that time a former professor of mine told me about his experience taking courses taught by West at Princeton University. "He presents as this guy who's all about activism and being on the streets with the people," he said, "but I've seen him spin academic arguments about philosophy and theology as complex as any other Ivy League philosopher." As you'll come to see—if you aren't familiar already—that is quite an accurate description of "Brother West."

Unlike some of the figures we'll explore in this book, West doesn't exist in historical obscurity or exclusively academic spaces. Rather, he's a prominent cultural figure who could be engaged with in any number of formats. He's appeared on popular television programming like *The Late Show* with David Letterman and *Anderson Cooper 365*, and starred in two of the films in *The Matrix* trilogy. He is a world-renowned scholar of philosophy, religion, and history who has held academic posts at such institutions as Yale, Harvard, and Princeton (the latter two being his alma maters for his baccalaureate, and his masters and doctoral degrees, respectively), among others. He's written or edited dozens of books, in addition to essays, articles, interviews, podcasts, and other forms of media. And we haven't even mentioned his activistic involvement with racial and social justice movements in the US yet.

West's work and legacy has long loomed over my career and—in the absolute best way possible—made me feel convicted for not having done more with my life. But even though I'll never be able to match the vastness of his résumé, he has accomplished in me what I believe to be his goal for all who engage his work: he's made me think deeply about critically important issues through the lens of poor, oppressed, and disenfranchised populations. For some, though, West and his work is approached with suspicion, not because of his liberationist ideas about race or his activism, but because of his sympathies toward socialism and Marxism.

His 1980 doctoral dissertation from Princeton was entitled "Ethics, Historicism, and the Marxist Tradition" and was later published under the title *The Ethical Dimensions of Marxist Thought*. His first book (published in 1982), *Prophesy Deliverance! An Afro-American Revolutionary Christianity*, is an attempt to "put forward a prophetic interpretation of the Christian tradition rooted in the Afro-American struggle against white supremacy, informed by progressive Marxist theory."[2] Such rhetoric, especially in a post-McCarthyism America, can still present as problematic for some. And it's okay to take issue with some figures' underlying philosophies and ideas, but we must *always* make a good-faith attempt at understanding them first.

We can critique West's Marxist ideology, but we can't ignore the similarities between West's quotation at the top of the chapter and the sentiments of the well-known, well-loved, well-celebrated figure of Martin Luther King Jr. Just as King spoke about the "giant triplets" of economic exploitation, militarism, and racism, so West has his own version, which corresponds surprisingly well: free-market fundamentalism, aggressive militarism, and escalating authoritarianism. Whether or not West had King in mind when writing about those things, we don't know, but both of their motivations are clear: resistance to social and political structures that lead to oppression of the poor and socially disempowered.

Those "most profound, seminal teachings of Christianity" West mentions above—which lend themselves to resistance against oppressive powers—are ones that he has taken to heart in his activism. He's been involved in advocacy for a wide breadth of issues including animal rights, labor unions, pro-Palestinian policy (which West claims led to his public and explosive resignation from Harvard in 2002) the economic exploitation of Wall Street, New York City stop-and-frisk policies, and, of course, racial injustice, among others. In most recent memory, West was among the protestors arrested in October of 2014 in the wake of the Ferguson Uprising following the police killing of Michael Brown. When asked by *CNN*'s Hala Gorani if he expected to be arrested

---

2. West, *Prophesy Deliverance!*, 5.

in Ferguson, he replied "I didn't go to give a speech; I went to go to jail."[3] For West, when current political and social pathways don't allow for social change, the only way to spotlight and reshape cultural opinion around issues of injustice is by showing up and taking part in acts of civil disobedience, even if it results in arrest.

Regardless of your thoughts about West's political alignment or specific pieces of his advocacy work, you need not look far to see that he's dedicated his life and career to bringing good news to the oppressed, binding up the brokenhearted, and proclaiming liberty to the captives and release to the prisoners, as a well-known passage from Isa 61 states. It's with these elements of prophetic Christianity in mind that West weighs American Christian fundamentalism and finds it wanting. With its "emphasis on personal conversion, individual piety, and philanthropic service" non-prophetic Christianity has "lost its fervor for the suspicion of worldly authorities and for doing justice in the service of the most vulnerable among us."[4]

For West, these components of prophetic Christianity are constitutive of Christianity *as such* for it to be authentic Christianity (which isn't dissimilar from the likes of James Cone's black theology). Personal conversion and individual piety aren't problematic in and of themselves but become problematic when they are the end-all-be-all of the Christian faith. If we're not living out our faith in service to the oppressed, brokenhearted, captives, and prisoners, then our faith is harmful at worst and incomplete at best.

REFLECT

1. I mention toward the beginning of the chapter that West is a popular and public intellectual who is visibly present in pop culture. If you were familiar with West before now, what was your impression of him? Has that impression changed at all? If you weren't familiar with West before reading this chapter, what's your first impression of him?

3. West, "Cornel West on Ferguson," 03:19.
4. West, *Democracy Matters*, 150.

2. Read again West's quote at the top of the chapter. We all bring our own definitions of "Christian fundamentalism" to the table, but how do you think it, despite differences in definitions, enables and justifies oppressive economic, militaristic, and authoritarian ideas in America?

3. While figures we've already discussed, like King and Cone, contend that Christianity ought to have social and political implications, they're relatively far removed from our contemporary context. How do you feel about the way West puts Christianity and radical politics, like Marxism, into conversation with one another? Do you think he's on the right track or does it make you uncomfortable? Why do you think you feel that way?

4. West endorses a "prophetic" Christianity which (similar to Cone) takes the poor and oppressed as the primary point of departure. Think about your own ministry or the ministry of your faith community: do you think it falls within the tradition of a "prophetic" Christianity? Why or why not? If not, what changes can you make to move closer to that particular expression of the Christian faith?

KEEP READING

Cornel West

Black Prophetic Fire. Boston: Beacon, 2014.
Brother West: Living and Loving Out Loud, a Memoir. Toronto: Smiley, 2010.
Democracy Matters: Winning the Fight against Imperialism. New York: Penguin, 2004.
The Ethical Dimensions of Marxist Thought. New York: Monthly Review, 1991.
Keeping Faith: Philosophy and Race in America. Oxfordshire, England: Routledge, 1993.
Prophesy Deliverance! An Afro-American Revolutionary Christianity. Louisville: John Knox, 2002.
Prophetic Fragments. Grand Rapids: Eerdmans, 1988.
Prophetic Thought in Postmodern Times. Monroe, ME: Common Courage, 1993.
Race Matters. Boston: Beacon, 1993.

Cornel West

Restoring Hope: Conversations on the Future of Black America. Boston: Beacon, 1997.

6

James Baldwin

The black and white confrontation, whether it be hostile, as in the cities and labor unions, or with the intentions of forming a common front and creating the foundations of a new society, as with the students and the radicals, is obviously crucial, containing the shape of the American future and the only potential of a truly valid American identity. No one knows precisely how identities are forged, but it is safe to say that identities are not invented: an identity would seem to be arrived at by the way in which the person faces and uses his experience.[1]

—James Baldwin (1924–1987)

I was hungry and you gave me food, I was thirsty and you gave me something to drink, I was a stranger and you welcomed me, I was naked and you gave me clothing, I was sick and you took care of me, I was in prison and you visited me.... Truly I tell you, just as you did it to one of the least of these who are members of my family, you did it to me.

—Matthew 25:35–36, 40

---

1. Baldwin, *No Name*, 189.

James Baldwin

ON THE MORNING OF September 15, 1963, Birmingham, Alabama—widely known as the most segregated city in America at the time—was shaken; physically, spiritually, and emotionally. That morning, at Sixteenth Street Baptist Church, dynamite that had been planted by four local Klansmen near the back of the church exploded, leaving four young African American girls dead. After the dust had settled, the injured were evacuated, and the limp bodies of the dead children carried out, one of the church's stained glass windows came into view to reveal a startling sight. A depiction of Jesus, with one hand raised in mid-conversation gesture and a shepherd's crook in the other, remained largely intact except for one particular piece: the face. In the explosion, the face of Christ had been blown out, lending a kind of strange anonymity to the otherwise immediately recognizable figure.

One week later, on the September 22 episode of the television program *Our Protestant Heritage*, a panel comprised of theologian Reinhold Niebuhr, activist Thomas Kilgore Jr., and author James Baldwin convened to try and make sense of the Birmingham tragedy. At the top of the discussion, when asked by Kilgore if the faceless Christ suggested to Baldwin any meaning about the Sixteenth Street Baptist Church bombing, Baldwin responded, saying,

> It suggests to me several meanings. If I was going to be cynical this morning, I'd say that the absence of the face is something of an achievement since we've been victimized so long by an alabaster Christ. And it suggests, much more seriously, something else, and to me it sums up the crisis we've been living through. If Christ has no face, then perhaps it is time that we, who, in one way or another, invented and are responsible for our deities, give him a new face; give him a new consciousness and make the whole ideal, the whole hope, of Christian love a reality. And as far as I can tell that has never really been a reality in the two thousand years since his assassination.[2]

---

2. Baldwin, "Meaning of the Birmingham Tragedy," 29:35. I'm indebted to Dr. Christopher Hunt for drawing my attention to this interview in a lecture he gave on Baldwin at the Walk Justly Conference at Manchester UMC in 2022 in St. Louis, Missouri.

To an extent, this statement is indicative of Baldwin's disposition toward religion, and Christianity in particular. An avid preacher in some of Harlem's charismatic congregations as a teenager, Baldwin became disillusioned with Christianity nearly as quickly as he was initiated into it. Not only did he begin to recognize the exploitative nature of the church's hierarchy as his pastors became wealthy on the tithes and offerings of the poor congregation, but also that it lacked a self-sacrificial attitude toward the white community that, according to his understanding, would be becoming of a follower of Christ: "What is the point, the purpose, of *my* salvation if it did not permit me to behave with love toward others, no matter how they behaved toward me? What others did was their responsibility, for which they would answer when the judgment trumpet sounded. But what *I* did was *my* responsibility, and I would have to answer, too."[3]

If you have an eye for patterns, you may be seeing one emerge thus far: *responsibility*. That's the theme that penetrates much of Baldwin's work, especially in regard to religion. You see only a couple examples of this here in his response to the Sixteenth Street Baptist Church bombing and his disappointment with organized religion. Those of us who subscribe to popular religious doctrines and claim membership in powerful religious organizations have an obligation to steward our theology responsibly. And if our theology is being utilized for oppressive ends, then it's *our* responsibility to either course-correct (as in Baldwin's sentiment about giving Christ a new face) or abandon ship altogether.

Baldwin even noticed these oppressive theologies taking root outside explicitly religious institutions and materials and didn't hesitate to hold them to account. His essay "Everybody's Protest Novel," a scathing critique of literature attempting to expound the oppression of African Americans, took issue largely with the religious and theological undertones of some popular writers' social analysis. Likely the most well-known work discussed in the essay, *Uncle Tom's Cabin*—the Antebellum-era novel by Harriet Beecher Stowe—was, according to Baldwin, "activated by what might be

---

3. Baldwin, *Fire Next Time*, 40, emphasis original.

called a theological terror, the terror of damnation . . . not different from that terror which activates a lynch mob." Such an assessment spring's from Baldwin's evaluation that the "virtuous rage of Mrs. Stowe is motivated by nothing so temporal as a concern for the relationship of men to one another . . . but merely by a panic of being hurled into the flames, of being caught in traffic with the devil."[4] In short, Stowe's interests lie not in the liberation of black people from slavery and oppression, nor in a cultural recognition of black humanity, but in a merely metaphysical salvation of the soul (which, according to Baldwin's reading of Stowe, meant a rejection of blackness and embrace of whiteness).

Baldwin's own attempt to push back against these theologies and regain control over popular religious language was what we might call an exercise in "theological anthropology." It was an effort to speak theologically about the nature of humanity and the relationship between the human and the divine. Already seen a bit above, this strategy is present elsewhere also. His play *The Amen Corner* tells the story of a pastor, Margaret Alexander, in a New York City church as she navigates issues of spirituality and morality in her family, her church, and herself. "I'm just now finding out what it means to love the Lord," Margaret says at the end of the play. "To love the Lord is to love all His children—all of them, everyone!—and suffer with them and rejoice with them and never count the cost."[5]

As is made plain here, for Baldwin, there's no distance between loving God and loving people. Loving God means loving humanity in all of its complication and messiness without giving in to the desire to either reduce people to a single facet of their identity *or* separate them from God altogether. Baldwin's solution to the misuse of theology in America's social dialogue was to take up the same sentiment Jesus puts forth in Matt 25: to identify God with those in need of care and justice in the world without regard for how it may affect us.

---

4. Baldwin, "Everybody's Protest Novel," 30.
5. Baldwin, *Amen Corner*, 88.

Extremists for Love

The list Jesus puts forth in this passage—the hungry, thirsty, stranger, naked, sick, and imprisoned—while not irrelevant to our contemporary context, is also not exhaustive. These could very well replace the face of Christ in the Sixteenth Street Baptist Church window, but there's no reason to preclude any of the faces of the black and brown people lynched by racist mobs and police departments in the last century. And what Baldwin teaches us is that it's the church's task to make sure that the new face of Christ isn't another of alabaster origin, but is one that reflects the oppressed of today's world so worthy to identify with the crucified Nazarene.

REFLECT

1. Consider Baldwin's response to the Sixteenth Street Baptist Church bombing and the issue of Christ's missing face in the window. How do those of us in the church (either as clergy, staff, or laity) contribute, as Baldwin says, to inventing and being responsible for our deity?

2. Baldwin became disillusioned with the Christian church due, in large part, to its seeming financial exploitation of the poor while pastors and religious leaders became wealthy. In what ways do you see your faith community attempting to utilize its finances equitably and responsibly? In what ways might you think it could be doing better?

3. In Baldwin's most popular and well-known work, *The Fire Next Time*, he says that "if the concept of God has any validity or any use, it can only be to make us larger, freer, and more loving. If God cannot do this, then it is time we got rid of him."[6] Do you agree? Why or why not? How does it make you feel to think about the idea of "getting rid" of God?

4. Matthew 25 is a text people have long looked to for inspiration in the fight against injustice, and Baldwin's own personal

---

6. Baldwin, *Fire Next Time*, 47.

theology seems to emulate a similar idea. How are you and your current ministries finding Christ in the poor and oppressed? Are your church's ministries geared toward these populations or merely designed for people already inside the church community?

5. "Responsibility" is a theme Baldwin utilizes throughout his work, specifically the responsibility of Christians for the ways their theologies are used. Think critically about your personal or denomination's theology; are there aspects of either that you think could be utilized for oppression instead of liberation? If so, how might they be reformed?

KEEP READING

James Baldwin

The Cross of Redemption: Uncollected Writings. Edited by Randall Kenan. New York: Pantheon Books, 2010.
The Fire Next Time. New York: Vintage International, 1993.
Go Tell It on the Mountain. New York: Vintage International, 2013.
Just Above My Head. New York: Dial, 1964.
Nobody Knows My Name: More Notes of a Native Son. New York: Dial, 1961.
No Name in the Street. New York: Dial, 1972.
Notes of a Native Son. Boston: Beacon, 2012.
The Price of the Ticket: Collected Nonfiction 1948–1985. New York: St. Martin's, 1985.

Marc Dudley

Understanding James Baldwin. Columbia: University of South Carolina Press, 2019.

Christopher Z. Hobson

James Baldwin and the Heavenly City: Prophecy, Apocalypse, and Doubt. East Lansing: Michigan State University Press, 2018.

Susan J. McWilliams

A Political Companion to James Baldwin. Edited by Susan J. McWilliams. Lexington: University Press of Kentucky, 2017.

Extremists for Love

Bill V. Mullen

James Baldwin: Living in Fire. London: Pluto, 2019.

7

Sojourner Truth

God is without end, and all that is good is without end. We shall never see God only as we seen Him in one another. He is a great ocean of love, and we live and move in Him as the fishes in the sea, filled with His love and spirit, and His throne is in the hearts of his people.[1]

—SOJOURNER TRUTH (1797–1883)

From one ancestor he made all nations to inhabit the whole earth, and he allotted the times of their existence and the boundaries of the places where they would live, so that they would search for God and perhaps grope for him and find him—though indeed he is not far from each one of us. For "in him we live and move and have our being"; as even some of your own poets have said, "For we too are his offspring."

—ACTS 17:26–27

"WHEN PEOPLE THINK ABOUT theologians, I want them to think about Sojourner Truth." That's what my friend Kate told me when we met over lunch to talk about this project. Kate wrote a large portion of her PhD dissertation on Sojourner Truth, so I knew she

---

1. Truth, "Letter," 201.

would be the perfect person to dialogue with about this particular chapter. And she's right: when people think about theologians, I don't assume their minds automatically go to someone like Sojourner Truth, but they should. Truth was a theologian in her own right who dealt critically with the biblical witness and was able to accurately articulate her theological ideas. Those ideas didn't emerge in a vacuum, though. They were nurtured and developed through her interaction with both the African religion of her parents and grandparents and the Dutch Protestantism prevalent in the community she was born into.

Truth—originally named Isabella and taking on the surnames of her various owners, before claiming a new name for herself later in life—was born into a slave family in New York in 1797. Her maternal grandparents had survived the brutally violent Middle Passage of the Transatlantic Slave Trade, making her a third-generation slave after her father, James, and mother, Elizabeth. The immediacy of her Christian surroundings, coupled with her family's collective memory of the African motherland and their religious roots, yielded to the young Isabella a spiritual amalgamation including, among other things, both Christian doctrine and African cosmology.

In her autobiographical *Narrative of Sojourner Truth* (produced with the assistance of a woman named Olive Gilbert on account of the fact that Truth never learned to read or write), Truth tells of her mother instructing her and her siblings, "My children, there is a God, who hears and sees you. . . . He lives in the sky, and when you are beaten, or cruelly treated, or fall into any trouble, you must ask help of him, and he will always hear and help you."[2] This instruction about a metaphysical God who intercedes in history provided a theological foundation for Isabella to build upon in her development as a religious leader *and* while navigating the experience of early American slavery. In fact, it was this very theological foundation that allowed Isabella to walk away—literally and figuratively—from the institution of slavery once and for all.

---

2. Truth, *Narrative*, 7. For more on Olive Gilbert and her relationship with Truth, see Washington, *Sojourner Truth's America*, 181–90.

After her owner failed to fulfill his promise of emancipation at the time he had previously communicated to her, Truth made the decision to escape, but was plagued by fear of leaving in the darkness of night *and* in the conspicuous light of day. It was amidst this mental anguish that she realized she could merely leave at dawn while the light was beginning to break through, but before people were stirring in the community. "Thank you, God, for *that* thought!" Truth exclaimed. After she collected some provisions and her infant child, she merely walked off from her master's house. "Turning her thoughts to God, her only help, she prayed him to direct her to some safe asylum," after which she was led to a Mr. Isaac S. van Wagener.[3] After being tracked down by her previous owner, Van Wagener paid the man off and—in the legal sense of the word—became Truth's legal master. However, that's not a title Van Wagener would tolerate: "there is but *one* master; and he who is *your* master is *my* master."[4]

While having experienced the various (and often competing) theological influences from both the religion of her enslavers and the religion of her mother, one thing for Truth was clear: the God she believed in was a *God of all*. Recalling a particularly spiritual vision, Truth experienced that "with all the suddenness of a flash of lightning . . . there was no place where God was not."[5] It was this same sense of God's vastness that accompanied Truth, over a decade later, when she elected to leave New York and travel west to "[testify] of the hope that was in her . . . [exhort] the people to embrace Jesus," and the like.[6] It was at this time that Truth decided

---

3. Truth, *Narrative*, 28–29.
4. Truth, *Narrative*, 30.
5. Truth, *Narrative*, 49.
6. Truth, *Narrative*, 80. Whereas we might think of this as a very straightforward explanation of preaching, Truth considered it the task of lecturing. As Hanch points out in *Storied Witness*, though, considering these activities within the category of "preaching"—and Truth as a "preacher"—helps us overturn a long patriarchal history of considering sermons to be undertaken exclusively by men. For more, see Hanch, *Storied Witness*, 111–48.

to no longer go by her given name, but instead, Sojourner, telling an acquaintance, "The Spirit calls me . . . and I must go."[7]

Thus began Truth's formal ministerial career, which would take her all over the country and lead her to converse with the likes of Abraham Lincoln, Elizabeth Cady Stanton, Frederick Douglass, and other near-legendary figures in American history. She spent her career preaching at religious gatherings, advocating for the abolition of slavery, and promoting women's rights. In a very real way, Truth was an early forerunner of "intersectional" thinkers and activists (much like Angela Davis discussed earlier and many we'll discuss later), extensively examining the unique injustices that happen at the intersection of both an oppressed gender identity *and* oppressed racial identity. Her most famous expression of this work comes in the form of her famous "Ar'n't I a Woman?" speech, given at a women's rights convention in Akron, Ohio, in 1851.[8]

At this event, Truth addressed the convention about the equality of women with men on three separate fronts: body, mind, and soul. She recalled her time as a slave and the physical work she was forced to carry out that was equal with any man's as well as reassured any suspicious listeners that "you need not be afraid to give us our rights for fear we will take too much." Her final rhetorical blow, though, comes at the end of her speech when discussing women's spiritual equality with men: "How came Jesus into the world? Through God who created him and the woman who bore him. Man, where was your part?"[9] If it's one thing Truth's career was defined by, it was boldness. Or as Margaret Washington puts it, Truth had a "defiant character."[10]

---

7. Truth, *Narrative of Sojourner Truth*, 80.

8. There are several different versions of the speech, and the exact transcript of Truth's words is disputed. For more on the various dimensions of the debate over Truth's words, see: Hanch, *Storied Witness*, 134–38; Koester, *We Will Be Free*, 103–7 and 149–51; Washington, *Sojourner Truth's America*, 224–29. To read the various transcripts of the speech, see Koester, *We Will Be Free*, 221–24.

9. Koester, *We Will Be Free*, 221–22.

10. Washington, *Sojourner Truth's America*, 229.

For Truth, the question wasn't which gender or race was superior to the other; instead, the question was—given that all people were created by the same God—why would people believe that any race or gender was superior in the first place? As we see at the top of the chapter, Truth believed that all people "live and move in him as fishes in the sea." And while those of us in the twenty-first-century church might not give much thought to this idea, it was certainly bold and defiant for many two hundred years ago during Truth's lifetime.

It was her faith, though, in a God both close enough to feel our sufferings and transcendent enough to overturn injustice and evil that motivated Truth to preach such a "defiant" message; a motivation that we might attribute to the working of this Holy Spirit. Hanch calls this divine work in Truth's life the Holy Spirit's *withness*—"including both the meaning of the Spirit within and the notion of bearing witness."[11] The "withness" of the Holy Spirit—and Truth's obedience to it—is what led Truth to hold up the bodies of slaves, women, and the poor to the people in power and claim with absolute conviction, "*we too* are his offspring."

REFLECT

1. Sojourner Truth and other black women preachers are not often thought about when we think about recalling theologians of the past. Why do you think that is? What assumptions do we have about who a theologian should be and what they do?

2. Like many of the slaves of her day, Truth never learned how to read or write, meaning she only ever interacted with Scripture and Christian history through listening and discussion. How do you think this experience affected Truth as she grew in her faith? What, if any, issues of justice do you see in people not being able to read or interact with the Bible on their own?

---

11. Hanch, *Storied Witness*, 112.

3. In this chapter, Truth is quoted saying, "there was no place where God was not." For many of us, this idea of a ubiquitous God is merely an intellectual exercise or acknowledgment, whereas for Truth it was a very literal reality. Having learned a bit about Truth, how do you see this idea manifesting in her life and faith?

4. In what ways can the church (both the church universal and your specific place of worship or ministry) learn from Truth's boldness and defiance in the face of injustice? Just as Truth asked the crowd difficult questions in her "Ar'n't I a Woman" speech, what difficult questions should we be asking people in power today?

KEEP READING

Sojourner Truth

The Narrative of Sojourner Truth. Edited by Margaret Washington. New York: Vintage Books, 1993.

Suzanne Pullon Fitch and Roseann M. Mandziuk

Sojourner Truth as Orator: Wit, Story, and Song. Westport, CT: Greenwood, 1997.

Kate Hanch

Storied Witness: The Theology of Black Women Preachers in 19th-Century America. Minneapolis: Fortress, 2022.

Nancy Koester

We Will Be Free: The Life and Faith of Sojourner Truth. Grand Rapids: Eerdmans, 2023.

Patricia C. and Frederick McKissack

Sojourner Truth: Ain't I a Woman? New York: Scholastic, 1992.

SOJOURNER TRUTH

Nell Irvin Painter
Sojourner Truth: A Life, A Symbol. New York: Norton, 1996.

Margaret Washington
Sojourner Truth's America. Chicago: University of Illinois Press, 2009.

8

John Brown

I, John Brown, am now quite certain that the crimes of this guilty land will never be purged away but with blood. I had, as I now think, vainly flattered myself that without very much bloodshed it might be done.[1]

—JOHN BROWN (1800–1859)

But thus says the LORD: Even the captives of the mighty shall be taken, and the prey of the tyrant be rescued; for I will contend with those who contend with you, and I will save your children. I will make your oppressors eat their own flesh, and they shall be drunk with their own blood as with wine.

—ISAIAH 49:25–26a[2]

IN AN AFRICAN AMERICAN newspaper called *The Chicago Defender*, the prolific black writer Langston Hughes published an article about John Brown on October 17, 1959—the centennial of an event known as the "Harpers Ferry Raid." It was this event, exactly a hundred years earlier, for which the white abolitionist

---

1. Nelson, *Old Man*, 278.
2. According to Jonathan F. Fanton and Richard Warch, this passage was marked in John Brown's personal Bible. See Fanton and Warch, *John Brown*, i.

John Brown

John Brown would be captured, tried, and hanged for conspiring to free black slaves in the South. In his centennial article, Hughes wrote, "The Civil War that freed the slaves really began with John Brown's Raid."[3]

Now, it's true that the Civil War started only two years following Brown's raid and subsequent hanging, but an important question we must confront is: If it's true that Brown played a key role in sparking the fire of the Civil War, *why don't more people know about him*? Why isn't he held up as a great hero of the movement for black freedom and the ending of slavery? The answer to those questions, one could conjecture, lies in the complicated and seemingly contradictory nature of John Brown's life and legacy.

Much like Nat Turner, whom we've already talked about here (and one of Brown's personal heroes), Brown's abolitionist and anti-racist sympathies were a direct result of his pious life of faith. In fact, as counterintuitive as it may seem to us, Brown was a *bona fide* Puritan with family roots in the New England colonies. Oftentimes—or most times, perhaps—when we think about the Puritans, we think about the stereotypically gentle, peace-seeking pilgrims who came over on the Mayflower. What we *don't* usually think about is a faith that inspires passionate, violent rebellion against injustice.

In spite of that, though, Brown's sincere hatred for the institution of slavery and his stoic acceptance of various heartbreaks throughout his life can be traced clearly to his religious belief. Brown was intensely influenced in his upbringing by an "unusual family atmosphere of fervent Calvinism and equally fervent Abolitionism."[4] This zeal sustained Brown amidst the death of children, failed business ventures, hunger, poverty, and, finally, his death at the gallows.

In October of 1859, Brown and a handful of men—including both black soldiers and white soldiers, and two of his own sons—took to the federal armory in Harpers Ferry, Virginia, with the intention of emptying it of its various weaponry and using them

---

3. Quarles, *Blacks on John Brown*, 121.
4. Reynolds, *John Brown, Abolitionist*, 23.

to arm fellow slaves and abolitionists. Despite any hope of success, Brown and his men were quickly overcome by opposing militant forces, resulting in several deaths (including both of his sons) and his own subsequent capture and imprisonment.

Despite the failure of the raid, Brown's faith remained steadfast. In a letter to his family, he wrote, "Under all these terrible calamities, I feel quite cheerful in the assurance that God reigns and will overrule all for his glory and the best possible good."[5] This outlook remained intact in the following weeks leading up to his death, and was recalled again and again under questioning about the raid. In an interview with various congressmen and reporters following his arrest, Brown makes reference to Scripture and the Christian tradition several times, twice invoking the "Golden Rule." When asked upon what principle he justified his acts, Brown responded, "Upon the Golden Rule. I pity the poor in bondage that have none to help them; that is why I am here; not to gratify any personal animosity, revenge, or vindictive spirit. It is my sympathy with the oppressed and the wronged that are as good as you and as precious in the sight of God."[6] Finally, just over a month after the Harpers Ferry raid, John Brown was hanged on December 2, 1859.

For many, the problem with Brown—again, like Nat Turner—isn't how radically he believed in the liberation of slaves or how fervently he believed in the Christian faith; it's the way his Christian faith spurned him on towards violent resistance. Debating the ethics of John Brown's actions, theological or otherwise, is not a new endeavor, not even for Brown himself. On several occasions (including the last written statement he would ever make, as is included at the top of the chapter) he showcased his wrestling with the idea of violent vs. nonviolent liberation. In that same interview with the congressmen and reporters we just mentioned, he states that he's resigned to the fact that "moral suasion is hopeless. I don't think the people of the slave States will ever consider the subject of

---

5. Reynolds, *John Brown, Abolitionist*, 384.
6. Stauffer and Trodd, *Meteor of War*, 125.

slavery in its true light till some other argument is resorted to than moral suasion."[7]

One gets the sense that Brown had wrestled with this question himself, and we know from other letters and writings that he did. And even if you find yourself struggling with the violent means of figures like Brown and Turner and others, we can't dismiss the fact that they make us think critically about the violence of Scripture. It's easy to give into the temptation to merely sidestep specific passages of the Bible that make us squeamish or suddenly thrust our black-and-white ethical frameworks into a gray fog, but that doesn't mean we should.

Isaiah 49 gives us the image of a very violent God, and it's from this God that Brown clearly took inspiration. But it's important to note that God's action in this passage isn't arbitrary. It's very intentionally carried out on behalf of the poor and oppressed who have been downtrodden by the powerful. While it might not always be comfortable to acknowledge, Brown's attempt to utilize the privilege and power he possessed as a white man in the Antebellum South and to overthrow the oppression of slavery—and his willingness even to die for it—isn't out of line with the biblical witness. To the contrary, his self-sacrificial example of love for his neighbor in the face of dire circumstances and opposition is quite Christlike. And if we're to actually acknowledge that, then we must entertain the same question W. E. B. DuBois asks in his biography of Brown: "Was John Brown simply an episode, or was he an eternal truth? And if a truth, how speaks that truth today?"[8]

REFLECT

1. Consider the questions asked at the very beginning of the chapter, when confronting the idea that Brown played an integral role in the sparking of the Civil War, yet very few people actually know his story. Why don't you think he's

---

7. Stauffer and Trodd, *Meteor of War*, 126.
8. DuBois, *John Brown*, 162.

taught more frequently in our schools, or discussed more often when talking about American history?

2. Throughout the chapter, there are references to similarities between John Brown and Nat Turner—both figures who engaged in violent rebellion against the institution of slavery. How do you think their legacies have been received differently based on the fact that Turner was black, and Brown was white?

3. In Brown's time, slavery was certainly considered a moral issue by those who subscribed to the principles of Abolitionism, but for many pro-slavery people, it was a political issue like any other. Think about the hot-button topics in our context today: how do you determine which issues are issues of morality versus issues exclusively of politics? Why do you think those two categories are so hard to pull apart sometimes?

4. In Brown's final written statement before his execution, he claimed that "the crimes of this guilty land will never be purged away but with blood." While this foreshadowed the Civil War, which would take place less than two years later, how are we to understand this today when we're still experiencing the symptoms of systemic racism, albeit in different forms? How do you understand Brown's statement in light of traditional Christian teaching, such as the blood of Christ that was spilt on the cross for the sins of humanity?

KEEP READING

H. W. Brands

The Zealot and the Emancipator: John Brown, Abraham Lincoln, and the Struggle for American Freedom. New York: Doubleday, 2020.

W. E. B. DuBois

John Brown. New York: Oxford University Press, 2007.

John Brown

Jonathan F. Fanton and Richard Warch
John Brown. Englewood Cliffs, NJ: Prentice-Hall, 1973.

Tony Horwitz
Midnight Rising: John Brown and the Raid That Sparked the Civil War. New York: Picador, 2012.

Truman Nelson
The Old Man: John Brown at Harper's Ferry. New York: Holt, Reinhart & Winston, 1973.

Stephen B. Oates
To Purge This Land with Blood: A Biography of John Brown. New York: Harper & Row, 1970.

Benjamin Quarles
Allies for Freedom and Blacks on John Brown. Cambridge, MA: Da Capo, 2001.

David S. Reynolds
John Brown, Abolitionist: The Man Who Killed Slavery, Sparked the Civil War, and Seeded Civil Rights. New York: Vintage Books, 2006.

Ted A. Smith
Weird John Brown: Divine Violence and the Limits of Ethics. Stanford, CA: Stanford University Press, 2015.

John Stauffer and Zoe Trodd
Meteor of War: The John Brown Story. Maplecrest, NY: Brandywine, 2004.

Barrie Stavis
John Brown: The Sword and the Word. Cranbury, NJ: A. S. Barnes, 1970.

9

The Black Panther Party

[Albert] Camus wrote that the revolutionary's "real generosity toward the future lies in giving all to the present." This, he says, grows out of an intense love for the earth, for our brothers, for justice. The Black Panther Party embraces this principle. By giving all to the present we reject fear, despair, and defeat. We work to repair the breaches of the past. We strive to carry out the revolutionary principle of transformation, and through long struggle, in Camus's words, "to remake the soul of our time."[1]

—Huey P. Newton (1942–1989)

All who believed were together and had all things in common; they would sell their possessions and goods and distribute the proceeds to all, as any had need. Day by day, as they spent much time together in the temple, they broke bread at home and ate their food with glad and generous hearts, praising God and having the goodwill of all the people.

—Acts 2:44–47a

---

1. Newton, *Revolutionary Suicide*, 358.

The Black Panther Party

In mid-2020, as the COVID-19 pandemic was raging and the riots following the murder of George Floyd were in full swing, my family moved from Pennsylvania back to our native St. Louis. That fall, I found myself working as an administrative assistant in a public high school library. As I cultivated relationships with the students and began to learn about their passions, anxieties, frustrations, and hopes, it became clear that they were far more aware of injustice and oppression on the basis of things like race and sexual identity and citizenship status than I was at their age. And as I fielded questions from them one day about the movement for black lives in America and shared my personal thoughts on what had happened to George Floyd in Minneapolis that summer, one student lifted up his voice and asked, "What do you know about the Black Panther Party?"

Surprised that a teenager even knew who the Panthers were, I carried on an ongoing dialogue in the weeks and months to come. I eventually even smuggled in some articles and reading materials for him that couldn't be found in the suburban school's library. Over the course of that year, one thing became obvious to me: young people were starting to ask the same questions that the Black Panther Party asked half a century ago. And while I didn't have all the answers about how to address systemic racism in twenty-first-century America, the least I could do was help these kids understand how a group of young, powerful black visionaries answered it in the past.

The Black Panther Party (originally The Black Panther Party for Self-Defense) was established in 1966 in Oakland, California, by Huey P. Newton and Bobby Seale as a collective dedicated to combating the brutality and harassment the black community frequently suffered at the hands of the local police department. The organization quickly grew into a network of branches and offices across the United States, with chapters spanning the coasts from California to New England. Far from being "paranoid extremists," as they're classified by historian Neil A. Hamilton (who also incorrectly claims they were founded in 1967 rather than October

1966),[2] the Panthers were keenly aware that "even with the passage of the Civil Rights Act [in 1964] and the Voting Rights Act in 1965—even as Jim Crow laws began to disappear—violence and racism persisted."[3]

As they began to organize the black community and formulate the Black Panther Party's platform, though, they were sure to emphasize that they were not mere militant reactionaries without structure or guidelines. Rather, the Panthers deeply valued discipline, education, and community transformation, and everything they did was for this end. While often caricatured as nothing more than a violent, black militia merely due to their willingness to defend themselves against racist attacks (especially when taken against the backdrop of Martin Luther King Jr.'s philosophy of nonviolence), the Panthers, in actuality, desired nothing more than to organize communities around mutual aid to one another. This manifested, most notably, in their "survival programs."

These programs—often differing from community to community based on an area's specific needs—included free breakfast for children (by far the most popular), free daycare centers so women could be a part of the Panthers' movement, free shoes and clothing, free ambulance and EMT service, free medical clinic and sickle-cell screenings, free bussing to prisons to visit family members, and liberation schools as an alternative to the public school system. These programs were far more than a metaphorical bandage on people's wounds to temporarily stop the bleeding. Instead, they were experiments in community progress and self-determination. Recognizing the injustices, disinvestment, and disenfranchisement that black communities had suffered, the Panthers' survival programs were meant to not only help people achieve a basic level of survival, but rather to help them *thrive*, so they could thereby aid in the transformation of entire communities.

Speaking of the survival programs, Ericka Huggins, who ran the Oakland Community School (founded by the Black Panther Party), said that "real change occurs, because if you give people

2. Hamilton, *Militias in America*, 14–15.
3. Bloom et al., *Freedom!*, 23.

a decent education and some nice clothing to wear and maybe a roof over their heads, that's a beginning. But the real change occurs within."[4] These programs, in a very real way, were revolutionary because they allowed people to move beyond striving for mere subsistence. Fred Hampton, the deputy chairman of the Illinois chapter of the party, said that "any program is revolutionary if it's an advancing program; revolution is change."[5]

The ideological roots of these programs and the Panthers' attempts at community transformation can be found in the "Ten Point Program"—a list of beliefs and demands laid out by the party. Among these points are decent housing, education that exposes the true nature of American history, exemption of black men from military service, and an end to police brutality and murder.[6] These demands, though, never came to pass.

It didn't take long for the federal government to officially demonize the party. In July of 1969, less than three years after the Panthers were established, FBI director J. Edgar Hoover claimed that the Black Panther Party represented "without question . . . the greatest threat to the internal security of this country."[7] The FBI's Counter Intelligence Program—or "COINTELPRO," for short—would eventually infiltrate the Panthers and plant informants in the organization, providing the information subsequently used to raid the Black Panthers' Illinois headquarters and assassinate Fred Hampton at only twenty-one years old (the subject of Shaka King's 2021 biopic, *Judas and the Black Messiah*).[8]

---

4. Bloom et al, *Freedom!*, 178.
5. Williams, *From the Bullet*, 95.
6. For a full list of the party's platform and programs, see Shames, *Black Panthers*, 14–15.
7. Bloom et al, *Freedom!*, 204.
8. The language of "assassination" is intentional. Reports indicate that not only did the FBI's plant within the BPP drug Hampton with a sleeping agent the night before the raid but also that the team that carried out the raid shot a total of ninety-nine bullets into the apartment where Hampton and others were sleeping, with only a single shot being returned. According to eyewitness testimony and autopsy evidence, Hampton was still alive after the shoot-out and assassinated at point-blank range in his bed by the officers. For more on

If there's one thing we can learn from the ancient church communities, it's that those in authority don't often take kindly to the loss of power and control. In Acts 2, we see a community holding "all things in common" and caring for one another "as any had need," and only two chapters later, in Acts 4, we see the apostles start to get arrested for this new message they're preaching. We need not look far to understand that the concept of community that the early church had is the same one that the Black Panthers had: a community where all gave according to their ability, and each received according to their need. While not always obvious or explicit in presentation, we would do well to take note of the Panthers' biblical vision for how we are to care for the poor and oppressed among us. After all, the kinds of people that the Black Panthers desired to help were the very same ones Jesus was concerned about. If the church could embrace this vision for community transformation and equity, and elect to consciously build its ministries around it rather than the desires of its insiders, it would not only bring itself into closer alignment with Scripture, but also foster revolutionary growth and change in the world around it.

REFLECT

1. As is mentioned during the chapter, the Black Panther Party has long been portrayed negatively due to their unwillingness to embrace Martin Luther King Jr.'s commitment to nonviolence. Regardless of whether or not you lived through the Panthers' era, what assumptions did you have about the Panthers before reading this chapter? Did they hold true, or were they challenged?

2. <u>Activity</u>: If you're able, do some additional research and find the full outline of the Black Panthers' Ten-Point Program. Read through each point and find a corresponding biblical

---

Hampton's murder, see National Archives, "Fred Hampton"; and Haas, *Assassination of Fred Hampton*.

passage. What parallels do you find between the Panthers' platform and the message(s) of Scripture?

3. Even if they weren't explicitly modeled after it, the Panthers' "survival programs" heavily mirrored the description of the early church's life together. Think about your immediate ministry context: What are the needs of *your* community? What kind of program(s) can you establish to help people "as any [have] need"?

KEEP READING

Mumia Abu-Jamal

We Want Freedom: A Life in the Black Panther Party. Cambridge, MA: South End, 2004.

Joshua Bloom; Jetta Grace Martin; Waldo E. Martin Jr.

Freedom! The Story of the Black Panther Party. Hoboken, NJ: Levine Querido, 2022.

Joshua Bloom and Waldo E. Martin Jr.

Black against Empire: The History and Politics of the Black Panther Party. Oakland: University of California Press, 2013.

John H. Bracey Jr.; August Meier; Elliot Rudwick (editors)

Black Nationalism in America. New York: Bobbs-Merrill, 1970.

Devin Fergus

Liberalism, Black Power, and the Making of American Politics 1965–1980. Athens: University of Georgia Press, 2009.

Jeffrey Haas

The Assassination of Fred Hampton: How the FBI and the Chicago Police Murdered a Black Panther. Chicago: Laurence Hill, 2019.

Judson L. Jeffries (editor)

Comrades: A Local History of the Black Panther Party. Bloomington: Indiana University Press, 2007.

Kekla Magoon

Revolution in Our Time: The Black Panther Party's Promise to the People. Somerville, MA: Candlewick, 2021.

Huey P. Newton

The Huey P. Newton Reader. Edited by David Hilliard and Donald Weise. New York: Seven Stories, 2002.

Revolutionary Suicide. New York: Penguin, 2009.

Jeffrey O. G. Ogbar

Black Power: Radical Politics and African American Identity. Baltimore: Johns Hopkins University Press, 2004.

Stephen Shames

The Black Panthers: Photographs. New York: Aperture Foundation, 2006.

Jakobi Williams

From the Bullet to the Ballot: The Illinois Chapter of the Black Panther Party and Racial Coalition Politics in Chicago. Chapel Hill: University of North Carolina Press, 2013.

10

Kendrick Lamar

I was baptized a few years ago. I got saved in a parking lot, like I said on "good kid, m.A.A.d city." The more I started going through my own things in life, my faith got put to the test, and I had to believe that God—my lord and savior, Jesus Christ—is real in my heart, and I can't run from that.[1]

—Kendrick Lamar (1987–)

A certain ruler asked him, "Good Teacher what must I do to inherit eternal life?" [Jesus responded,] "Sell all that you own and distribute the money to the poor, and you will have treasure in heaven; then come, follow me." But when he heard this, he became sad; for he was very rich. Jesus looked at him and said, "How hard it is for those who have wealth to enter the kingdom of God! Indeed it is easier for a camel to go through the eye of a needle than for someone who is rich to enter the kingdom of God."

—Luke 18:18, 22–25

---

1. Lewis, *Promise That You Will*, 17.

Extremists for Love

THE FIRST THING YOU hear on Kendrick Lamar's sophomore album (and first major record label offering), entitled *good kid, m.A.A.d city*, is the sound of a VHS tape being inserted into a VCR, followed by a dated-sounding recording of what's commonly referred to as "The Sinner's Prayer."[2] Not necessarily what you would expect at the top of a rap album that's not marketed as being explicitly religious, right? But it's exactly that unexpectedness that lends itself to Lamar's brilliance.

Lamar (legally Kendrick Lamar Duckworth) was raised in the late 1980s and early 1990s amidst the unrest following the police beating of Rodney King, and has publicly recalled his childhood's close proximity to poverty, drugs, and gang violence. In a 2015 interview with *NPR Music*, Lamar tells of the first time he witnessed a murder as a child when a drug dealer was killed in front of his apartment.[3] It was this cultural environment that fostered the young Lamar, and which is constantly called back to in his lyrics.[4]

Unlike many of his friends and family members, though, Lamar escaped his impoverished upbringing thanks to the success he found in music. One of the most successful and important rappers in a generation, Lamar has won seventeen Grammy awards and has been nominated forty-seven times (as of this writing).[5] In addition to an already impressive trophy case, in 2018 Lamar received the Pulitzer Prize in music for his masterful album, *DAMN.*—the first non-jazz or non-classical album ever to be given the accolade—undoubtedly legitimizing his music to a broader audience than would have previously given it the time of day. The album was awarded the prestigious prize for being "a virtuosic song collection unified by its vernacular authenticity and rhythmic dynamism that offers affecting vignettes capturing the complexity of modern African-American life."[6]

---

2. Lamar, "Sherane."
3. Lamar, "I Can't Change."
4. See Lamar, "HUMBLE."; and "DNA."
5. Grammy Awards, "Kendrick Lamar."
6. Pulitzer Prizes, "DAMN."

This complexity that Lamar so brilliantly portrays includes the realities of police brutality, class, gang wars, drugs, the prison industrial complex, and, of course, a deep-running spirituality and religious character that never ceases to show up in Lamar's lyrical genius. In his track "How Much a Dollar Cost" from the *To Pimp a Butterfly* album—famously claimed by Barack Obama as his favorite song of 2015[7]—we see Lamar tell the story of an interaction with a homeless man at a gas station who asks him for a dollar. Despite Lamar's financial success, he refuses to assist him. After Lamar and the man finish quarreling over the dollar he asked for, the homeless man reveals himself as God, sparking a spiritual crisis for Lamar at being confronted by the divine with his own selfishness. The song ends with an indication of redemption, though, as we hear what we might assume to be Lamar's inner dialogue asking for an opportunity to change and make right his wrong.[8]

Not only does this interaction invoke images of Matt 25 and the "anonymous" Christ who comes to the world embodied in "the least of these," but it also parallels figures like the rich young ruler from the synoptic gospels who became deeply saddened by Jesus' charge to sell all his belongings and distribute the money to the poor. And this biblical allusion isn't confined to merely this one song. In his track "DNA." on the *DAMN.* album, Lamar essentially articulates a doctrine of original sin,[9] and elsewhere, he engages the problem of suffering[10] and proposes a profoundly biblical eschatology, or doctrine, of last things.[11]

Though these religious references appear often, they're always in conversation with wider social issues like economic inequality, governmental corruption, and systemic racial injustice. At the end of his track "The Blacker the Berry" he even makes explicit reference to Trayvon Martin—the unarmed, black teenager killed in Florida in 2012 whose death ignited the Black Lives Matter

7. Platon, "Kendrick Lamar."
8. Lamar, "How Much."
9. Lamar, "DNA."
10. Lamar, "FEAR."
11. Lamar, "Alright."

movement. In fact, the chorus of his song "Alright" became a rallying cry during Black Lives Matter protests across the country.

His most recent album, though, carries perhaps the most stark religious imagery to date. The cover art of *Mr. Morale and the Big Steppers* features Lamar standing in what appears to be a run-down bedroom, holding a child and donning a crown of thorns with a breastfeeding mother in the background. As if the religious depiction wasn't clear enough from the album cover, the lyrics also continue to be saturated with biblical and theological language. His track "Crown" makes clear allusions to both the crown of thorns Lamar is seen wearing on the cover, and to Luke 12:48, "From everyone to whom much has been given, much will be required; and from the one to whom much has been entrusted, even more will be demanded."[12] In "Savior," he addresses the temptation to embrace the messianic character people have portrayed him as,[13] and in "Mother | Sober," he grapples with the concept of truth and his own struggles of faith amidst family crises.[14] Given the image on the cover of the album and many of the references made lyrically in his songs, Lamar continues to provide his listeners commentary on the frailty of human nature, the relationship between doubt and faith, and the fact that this broken world marred by suffering isn't the only possible world.

No matter which album you might pick up, you'll find Lamar calling for moral and spiritual transformation—of both oneself *and* wider society—in some form or fashion. Much like Jesus' interaction with the rich young ruler in Luke 18, Lamar's music stands as a constant reminder that no matter how much wealth, power, or privilege we acquire, we must accept both that we're never absolved of our responsibility to the poor or oppressed, nor should we become messianic and confuse ourselves with the divine. While we may not necessarily think of an artist's lyrics and records as sources of theological inquiry and critique, the church would do well to remember that it doesn't have a monopoly on

12. Lamar, "Crown."
13. Lamar, "Savior."
14. Lamar, "Mother | Sober."

who can speak about God, nor how that speech is carried out. Perhaps Fordham University professor Kathryn Reklis said it best in her 2018 article, featured in *The Christian Century*, when she said that Lamar "may be one of our greatest living public theologians."[15]

REFLECT

1. While Lamar's work masterfully weaves together religious ideas, moral responsibility, and the complicated nature of race in America, he's certainly not the only musical artist to produce socially conscious music. Who are some other singers or musicians you can think of who tackle difficult topics in their music? Why do you think it's important for pop culture figures to address these issues?

2. <u>Activity</u>: Select a well-known hymn or song from your tradition that is commonly utilized in corporate worship and read through the song's lyrics. Do you find that this song interacts with ideas of social justice or Christianity's moral responsibility? Do you think it's important for such ideas to be communicated through song in the worship space? If so, what changes to your worship might you suggest be made so as to musically accommodate such ideas?

3. As is noted above, Lamar makes a distinction between our responsibility to work towards eradicating injustice and the idea that we can ever achieve that all by ourselves. How do you see these two ideas as different? What does it mean to do the work of social justice without becoming "messianic"?

4. In the story of the rich young ruler from Luke 18, we see someone who has so idolized his own wealth and privilege that it warps his ideas around religion, community, and responsibility—a reality Lamar deals with constantly in his albums. How do you think wealth and privilege (particularly that of white people) affects the way race is understood in

15. Reklis, "Kendrick Lamar," 61.

America? What can the church do to unseat these idols and strip away their power in society?

KEEP READING

Miles Marshall Lewis

Promise That You Will Sing about Me: The Power and Poetry of Kendrick Lamar. New York: St. Martin's, 2021.

Marcus J. Moore

The Butterfly Effect: How Kendrick Lamar Ignited the Soul of Black America. New York: Atria, 2020.

KEEP LISTENING

Kendrick Lamar

good kid, m.A.A.d city. Jan. 2012. Aftermath/Interscope Records.
To Pimp a Butterfly. Mar. 2015. Aftermath/Interscope Records
DAMN. Apr. 2017. Aftermath Interscope Records.
Mr. Morale and the Big Steppers. May 2022. Aftermath/Interscope Records.

11

Harriet Tubman

I had crossed the line. I was free; but there was no one to welcome me to the land of freedom. I was a stranger in a strange land; and my home, after all, was down in Maryland; because my father, my mother, my brothers, and sisters, and friends were there. But I was free, and they should be free. I would make a home in the North and bring them there, God helping me.... I said to the Lord, "I'm going to hold steady on you, and I know you'll see me through."[1]
—Harriet Tubman (ca. 1820–1913)

You are a hiding place for me; you preserve me from trouble; you surround me with glad cries of deliverance. Selah. I will instruct you and teach you the way you should go; I will counsel you with my eye upon you.
—Psalm 32:7–8

Besides Martin Luther King Jr., with whom we started at the beginning of this book, Harriet Tubman is probably the only other figure in the table of contents whom I can say with relative

---

1. Bradford, *Scenes in the Life*, 20.

certainty that most—if not all—of my readers will be familiar with. That being said, though, the knowledge I gained about Tubman from the education of my upbringing was truncated, bland, and largely devoid of the boldness of spirit that animated her life (much like that of King). This spirit, though sometimes lost in the few photographic images we have of Tubman as an aging woman, first reared its head when she was but a child.

Born Araminta "Minty" Ross (later taking the name of her mother, Harriet, upon securing her freedom) in Maryland, she began being "hired out" to various people to perform housekeeping or childcare duties as young as five years old. She later recalled to her biographer and others that her youthfulness didn't serve to protect her from the harsh treatment of her owners, and that whippings and punishments were doled out on a regular basis.[2] But this harsh treatment never dampened her tenacity.

Around the age of thirteen, when working as a field hand, she noticed a fellow slave leaving his work and heading toward town. When the overseer followed him, so did Araminta. Upon being caught up to and verbally threatened with a whipping, the slave ran. But before the overseer could follow, the young Minty put herself in the doorway and blocked the path between the slave and his abuser. So, in a fit of rage, the overseer picked up a small weight off the store's counter and threw it at the slave, only for it to fall short and strike Minty in the head. From that point on, she suffered "somnolency [sic]" and was prone to a kind of "stupor or lethargy" which would come over her randomly and regularly for the rest of her life.[3]

As can be seen, even from childhood there were two things Tubman didn't fear risking her life for: others and freedom. This fearlessness served her well when, in 1849, she escaped her enslavement and headed north to Pennsylvania without the aid of either a guide or her then-husband, John Tubman, a freeman she had married five years earlier. It was on the other side of this

2. Clinton, *Harriet Tubman*, 17–20.
3. Bradford, *Harriet*, 15 and 109.

journey that our subject, once Araminta Ross and then Araminta Tubman, assumed her final identity: Harriet Tubman.

This fearlessness wasn't born within a vacuum, though. Tubman maintained a fierce, steadfast faith—developed both through her heavily Methodist milieu and the African spirituality of her ancestors—for her entire life, which heavily influenced her outlook on the trials and tribulations of the world. In her book *Bound for the Promised Land*, Kate Clifford Larson correctly assesses that "Tubman's religiosity was unquestionably rooted in powerful Methodist evangelical teachings and was also a mystical and deeply personal spiritual experience."[4]

This faith continued to serve Tubman as she entered into her work as a "conductor" on the legendary Underground Railroad (UGRR). Thomas Garrett, a fellow abolitionist and UGRR agent, noted in a letter to Tubman's biographer about her uncompromising religious life: "[Tubman] has more confidence in the voice of God, as spoken directly to her soul . . . and he talked with her every day of her life, and she has declared to me that she felt no more fear of being arrested by her former master, or any other person, when in his immediate neighborhood, than she did in the State of New York or Canada, for she said she never [*sic*]ventured only where God sent her, and her faith in a Supreme Power truly was great."[5] And upon the passing of the Fugitive Slave Act of 1850, which required local authorities in free states to aid Southern slaveowners in pursuing their escaped slaves, Tubman felt overwhelmingly called by God to the work of guiding slaves along the "liberty lines" of the UGRR.

As the Northern states were no longer considered safe for escaped slaves due to the Fugitive Slave Act, most of Tubman's "cargo" was smuggled out of the United States entirely and into Canada. While historically unclear, some estimates venture that Tubman saved as many as three hundred slaves, while others claim it was upwards of seventy. Likewise, as Tubman's slave abductions impacted the Southern economy of several communities, some

---

4. Larson, *Bound for the Promised Land*, 44.
5. Larson, *Bound for the Promised Land*, 169.

reports claim there was a prize of $40,000 placed on Tubman's head, while others put it as low as $12,000.[6] Regardless of the exact numbers, though, it's clear that Tubman's deep, abiding commitment to the liberation of slaves was her life's calling.

And though her work on the UGRR is her most well-known claim to fame, her work didn't stop there. She was acquaintances with John Brown, Sojourner Truth, and Frederick Douglass; she took an active role in the Civil War on behalf of the Union; she raised funds for various schools and hospitals; she supported Susan B. Anthony and Elizabeth Cady Stanton in the women's suffrage movement; and, in her more senior years, devoted herself to establishing "a separate charitable institution . . . for the needy and neglected of her race."[7]

Over the course of this incredibly varied life, Tubman was addressed many different ways: Araminta, Minty, Harriet, General Tubman (by John Brown). But her courage in the face of injustice and oppression as she sought to deliver people from slavery earned her a specifically biblical moniker of special import to the early slave communities in America: *Moses*. As Sarah Bradford, her biographer, said, "Though the results of her unexampled heroism were not to free a whole nation of bonds-men and bonds-women, yet this object was as much the desire of her heart, as it was of that of the great leader of Israel. Her cry to the slave-holders, was ever like his to pharaoh, 'Let my people go!' and not even he imperiled life and limb more willingly, than did our courageous and self-sacrificing friend."[8]

As was the case with her biblical namesake, Tubman's faith was marked by an uncompromising conviction that the God she served was a God who sought to deliver captives to freedom. While at one time it was the Israelites in Egypt, so in her time was

---

6. For a thorough discussion of these disputed numbers, see Humez, *Harriet Tubman*, 349–52.

7. Clinton, *Harriet Tubman*, 206. For a more thorough discussion of all Tubman's post-UGRR work, see Larson, *Bound for the Promised Land*, 191–202.

8. Bradford, *Harriet*, 3–4.

it black slaves in America. And while the oppression of black and brown people continues to exist in America, albeit in new forms, so those of us who follow the same God of Moses and Tubman must *also* have a vested interest in that same task of deliverance. While allowing our conceptions of God, personal piety, and moral formation to grow and evolve over time might be intimidating, we can't ignore the model we find in this Moses-figure of a deeply subversive and political faith that refuses to become actionless and apathetic in the face of injustice.

REFLECT

1. At the top of the chapter, I mention my own experience learning about Tubman and how (similar to learning about MLK as a child) it was "truncated" and "bland." Your experience may have been much the same. Why do you think the American educational system tends to "whitewash" these important figures in the history of black liberation?

2. Tubman was characteristically fearless in the face of danger, even from a young age (as can be seen above in the story of her thirteen-year-old self standing between a fellow slave and the overseer who wished to harm him). This fearlessness was born, at least in part, out of a fierce faith and belief that God would "see [her] through." How does this relate to the faith of other figures you've read about thus far in this book?

3. Tubman was often referred to as the "Moses of her people." Reread Exod 3 and Exod 14; what similarities do you note between Moses' story and Tubman's story?

4. Tubman worked for the liberation of slaves in the American South with the same demand as Moses: "Let my people go!" While for Tubman, this was a demand for the literal unshackling of human bodies from plantations, what might it look like today for us to demand that black Americans be "let go"? In what ways are black Americans still shackled?

KEEP READING

Sarah Bradford

Harriet: The Moses of Her People. New York: Lockwood, 1886.
Scenes in the Life of Harriet Tubman. Auburn, NY: W. J. Moses, 1869.

Catherine Clinton

Harriet Tubman: The Road to Freedom. New York: Little, Brown, 2004.

Jean M. Humez

Harriet Tubman: The Life and the Life Stories. Madison: University of Wisconsin Press, 2003.

Kate Clifford Larson

Bound for the Promised Land: Harriet Tubman, Portrait of an American Hero. New York: Ballantine, 2004.

12

Ella Baker

On what basis do you seek to organize people? Do you start to try to organize them on the fact of what you think, or what they are first interested in? You start where the people are. Identification with people.[1]

—Ella Baker (ca. 1903–1986)

But speaking the truth in love, we must grow up in every way into him who is the head, into Christ, from whom the whole body, joined and knit together by every ligament with which it is equipped, as each part is working properly, promotes the body's growth in building itself up in love.

—Ephesians 4:15–16

Anyone who has spent even a little time in the church—either as an attendee, a volunteer leader, or a staff person—can attest that very little happens without significant planning. Sunday morning worship, community service programs, small groups and Bible studies, children's Sunday school, and everything else takes meticulous organization and human power to make happen.

1. Riggs, *Can I Get a Witness?*, 165.

Extremists for Love

The problem, though, is that unless you've spent time behind the scenes doing the work, you might be prone to believe that it all comes together rather effortlessly and, thus, you're not needed. But, of course, that's typically far from the truth.

Likewise, social movements do not spontaneously fall into place such that people automatically feel empowered to use their voices and know exactly how to do that. However, for those of us who haven't spent much—if any—time doing the work of community organization, it may very well feel that way. Especially in the era of social media where information spreads rapidly and plans for protests or demonstrations can be quickly put into action, we might be prone to assume that very little effort is required for such work. But if we truly believed that, we would be sorely mistaken—both about the nature of organizing today and (especially) in the past.

It's in this kind of thankless, behind-the-scenes work of bringing like-minded people together and helping them see the sources of oppression around them that Ella Baker thrived. Acutely aware of these sources of oppression even in childhood, Baker reportedly struck a white boy across the face at the age of six for calling her the N-slur—a boldness inherited from her parents and grandparents (racial justice warriors in their own rights, including her grandfather who was a pastor).[2] It was this passion for dignity and worth of all people that would lead Baker into the work of organizing in the first place. In the 1930s, Baker was living in New York City when the Great Depression swung in and hit hard. Along with her coworker and boss at the *Negro National News*, George Schuyler, Baker formed the Young Negroes' Cooperative League (YNCL) and began organizing "buying clubs" and "cooperative ventures" among the black community. These co-ops "helped mitigate devastation of the Depression and increased social and political analysis within Black communities."[3]

From here, Baker joined the National Association for the Advancement of Colored People (NAACP) doing nationwide organizing on behalf of the association. It was during this time that

---

2. Dallard, *Ella Baker*, 10.
3. Ross, *Witnessing and Testifying*, 39.

Baker began to formulate her vision for what some have articulated as "participatory democracy": a "complex of ideas . . . bringing together in a new formulation the traditional appeal of democracy with an innovative tie to broader participation."[4] In short, the trajectory of Baker's work as she traveled around the country, organizing people around specific problems, aimed to establish for black communities the foundational vision of democracy: that *all* should have a fair say in the construction of society—a mentality which would pay dividends in her future work during the height of the Civil Rights Movement.

While Baker's work for the NAACP and her prior experience with the YNCL stand on their own as achievements in the fight for racial justice, Baker is most well-known for her work with the Southern Christian Leadership Conference (SCLC) and the Student Nonviolent Coordinating Committee (SNCC—pronounced "snick"). She was extensively involved in the SCLC—the organization of pastors and religious leaders for whom Martin Luther King Jr. was the face—even being its primary administrator and organizer at times. For how important and prolific the SCLC was, though, it wasn't without its problems. Not only were there certain issues of sexism, being an organization made up and led almost entirely by male clergy (a likely reason Baker was never named the SCLC's executive director), but its idealistic emphasis on King's vision and personality in lieu of strategic leadership presented roadblocks that Baker didn't foresee clearing. In other words, "the [SCLC's] emphasis on charismatic ministerial leadership was similarly at odds with her view of how organizations should be built to empower people to seek social change."[5] It was upon this realization that Baker began noticing the movement of young people carrying out lunch counter sit-ins; young people who, as Baker foresaw, could be organized.

In response to the growing number of sit-ins and their impact, Baker called together a conference with representatives from various geographical areas and colleges to form SNCC. SNCC differed

---

4. Mueller, "Ella Baker," 51.
5. Mueller, "Ella Baker," 62.

from the SCLC in several ways, but primary among them was that "in SCLC, the organization revolved around King; in SNCC, the leadership was group-centered. . . . A basic goal was to make it unnecessary for the people to depend on a leader, for them to be strong themselves."[6] Baker's primary concern across the spectrum of her career, as can be seen in her quote at the top of this chapter, wasn't power or privilege, but *people*. And as a racial justice leader, one might say that she did everything she could to work herself out of a job. She believed in giving the work of justice over to the community and the people willing to come together in the fight.

This idea shouldn't be foreign to us in the church. When we look at the way Moses organized the Israelites in the Old Testament; when we look at the way Jesus deployed his followers to preach, teach, and heal; when we look at the early Christian communities in the book of Acts and how they held all things in common and each took part in the church's ministry, we begin to see patterns of social structure incredibly similar to the "participatory democracy" that Baker embodied in her work. The church could stand to learn from Baker's example and her effort to always bring people along and make them self-sufficient.

To use Paul's language, "For just as the body is one and has many members, and all the members of the body, though many, are one body, so it is with Christ."[7] Baker saw this "body" for what it was: various experiences, gifts, and skills that could do amazing things when they *worked together*. And it's in this working together that, as our Ephesians passage says, the body can "build itself up in love." Only when all feel empowered to share their gifts and work horizontally across the spectrum of the human life to collaborate and cooperate for the purpose of justice (rather than adhering to arbitrary hierarchies) can the body of Christ start to become what God wants it to be.

---

6. Mooney and West, "Ella Baker," 198.
7. 1 Cor 12:12.

Ella Baker

REFLECT

1. Think about your immediate faith context—whether it be a church, parachurch organization, or some other type of ministry community—and consider the week-to-week programming that takes place. To what extent do people need to be organized in a communal way to make that programming happen? Now put yourself in the shoes of a black woman living amongst the racial hostility of the Jim Crow South; how much harder would it be to organize people around important issues in that context than the one you currently occupy?

2. Baker advocated for a kind of horizontalism and mutual empowerment in which the leadership of social movements was instilled into communities versus into a hierarchy or a single person's vision. What do you see as the benefits and drawbacks of this model? How does it compare to your ministry context?

3. Despite the Southern Christian Leadership Conference (SCLC) being an ecumenical organization of clergy and other ministerial leaders, it had clear issues of sexism among its ranks—a reality Baker was directly impacted by. Do you see your organization or denomination struggling with this (or a similar) issue? How might you be able to use your voice to advocate on behalf of the women (and other gender-variant individuals) in your organization or denomination?

4. Judging from what we see in the book of Acts and other areas of Scripture, the early Christian and Jewish communities seemed to be hinting at the kind of "participatory democracy" that Baker advocated. What changes could we be making—even at the local church level—to better reflect this structure meant to give each person ownership over the vision and work of the community?

KEEP READING

Vicki L. Crawford; Jacqueline Anne Rouse; Barbara Woods (editors)

Women in the Civil Rights Movement: Trailblazers and Torchbearers 1941–1965. Indianapolis: Indiana University Press, 1993.

Shyrlee Dallard

Ella Baker: A Leader behind the Scenes. Englewood Cliffs, NJ: Silver Burdett, 1990.

James W. Mooney and Thomas R. West (editors)

To Redeem a Nation: A History and Anthology of the Civil Rights Movement. St. James, NY: Brandywine, 1993.

Marcia Y. Riggs (editor)

Can I Get a Witness? Prophetic Religious Voices of African American Women, An Anthology. Maryknoll, NY: Orbis, 1997.

Rosetta R. Ross

Witnessing and Testifying: Black Women, Religion, and Civil Rights. Minneapolis: Fortress, 2003.

13

Malcolm X

Policies change, and programs change, according to time. But objective never changes. You might change your method of achieving the objective, but the objective never changes. Our objective is complete freedom, complete justice, complete equality, by any means necessary.[1]

—Malcolm X (ca. 1925–1965)

Listen, I will tell you a mystery! We will not all die, but we will all be changed, in a moment, in the twinkling of an eye, at the last trumpet. For the trumpet will sound, and the dead will be raised imperishable, and we will be changed. For this perishable body must put on imperishability, and this mortal body must put on immortality.

—1 Corinthians 15:51–53

In the preface to *Malcolm X Speaks*—the well-known collection of Malcolm X's mature writings and speeches from which the quote at the top of this chapter is taken—editor and activist George Breitman assesses X as "one of the most misunderstood

---

1. X, "At the Aubudon," 116.

and misrepresented men of our time."[2] Unfortunately, I'm not sure the tide has shifted on that sentiment since Breitman offered it up in 1966, the year after X was assassinated. Just a few short years ago, I overheard a high school-aged student making comment on X as "a bad man who promoted violence"; such is the narrative endorsed by many schools in the American education system, I suppose.

As we've hopefully gotten into the habit of by this point in the book, though, we should be willing to critically investigate this kind of wholesale condemnation when it's attributed to a black freedom fighter in American history. Recalling how the Black Panther Party was smeared by J. Edgar Hoover, and how the Panthers' Illinois chairman, Fred Hampton, was assassinated by officers within the FBI's COINTELPRO, it shouldn't surprise us if the historical narrative of X's legacy was shaped by powers with a vested interest in anti-blackness. And like many of the others discussed in this book, there was indeed an FBI file dedicated to X which was hundreds of pages long; an investment of time and resources also made during the Hoover era.

But X's work as a radical black activist didn't happen randomly; it was nurtured amongst his upbringing to two parents—Earl and Louise Little (a surname he shared until later adopting the religiously significant "X" as an adult)—who were deeply entrenched in the political struggles of the day and were keenly invested in the philosophy of Jamaican activist Marcus Garvey. This upbringing, though, didn't dissuade X from seeking out lucrative-yet-illegal methods of putting food on the table. At one point, a twenty-year-old Malcolm was arrested for breaking into houses and sentenced to eight to ten years in prison. It was during this stint, though, that X would discover the Islamic faith.

First introduced by his brother, Reginald, during a visit to the prison, X found the black Islamic sect that his siblings had joined, Nation of Islam (NOI), to be compelling. NOI preached a "black nationalist message of racial pride, a rejection of integration, and self-sufficiency" and condemned "all-white institutions, including

2. Breitman, "Foreword," viii.

Christianity," though they're probably most well-known for their depiction of "all whites, without exception, as devils."[3] Despite the obvious problems with wide, sweeping declarations such as these, when taken against the backdrop of black oppression in America, an organization being willing to say what was often only being thought was likely a breath of fresh air for the young Malcolm. And it was shortly after this conversion that he would reject his surname, "Little," and take on the enigmatic "X," "which represented his unknown African name and symbolized the heritage that had been stolen from him."[4]

By the late 1950s, X had climbed the ranks of the NOI and become its chief spokesperson; a position centered in the public eye and tasked with conveying the central tenets of the NOI's particular brand of Islam. These fundamental teachings, though, were categorically opposed to those being popularized by Martin Luther King Jr. at the time. Whereas King preached nonviolent resistance, X preached resistance "by any means necessary"; whereas King welcomed in whites who were sympathetic to the cause of racial justice, X derided all whites as devils; whereas King taught integration, X taught separation.[5] In a way, this comparison to King was mutually affective. On the one hand, it led to a kind of lukewarm embrace of King and his specific school of thought around nonviolence since—as far as the general public could tell—the alternative to him was a group willing to engage in violence. On the other hand, it led to a demonization of X *precisely because* he didn't decry violence as a means to liberation (despite the hypocrisy of the American state utilizing regular and widespread violence against blacks).

X remained steadfast in these convictions from his time of conversion well into adulthood. There was a definitive shift, however, in 1964 (the year before his assassination) when X made a pilgrimage to the Islamic holy land of Mecca. This trip, known as

3. Marable, *Malcolm X*, 77–78.
4. Myers, *Malcolm X*, 85.
5. For more information specifically about the way King and X each utilized the media, see Payne and Payne, *Dead Are Arising*, 376–418.

the *hajj*, is one of the five pillars of Islam and is considered a sacred obligation which all Muslims must undertake at least once in their lives (assuming they have the means to do so). But it was on this trip that, in X's own words, "what I have seen, and experienced, has forced me to re-arrange much of my thought-patterns previously held, and to toss aside some of my previous conclusions."[6]

Upon embarking on the pilgrimage, X found himself surrounded by Muslims of all different colors and ethnicities, including the white-skinned, blue-eyed people he had long decried as devils, who all shared the hajj together without discrimination or judgment: "a spirit of unity and brotherhood that my experiences in America had led me to believe could never exist between white and nonwhite."[7] Afterward, though, X would be a changed man. As much can be seen in his rhetoric immediately before and immediately after the pilgrimage.

On April 3, a mere ten days before his trip, he gave his famous "The Ballot or the Bullet" speech, in which he called on the powers that be with a demand for black voting rights, followed by the warning, "it'll be ballots, or it'll be bullets. It'll be liberty, or it will be death. The only difference about this kind of death—it'll be reciprocal."[8] Less than two months later, on May 23, he gave a speech in Chicago where he said, "In the past, I have permitted myself to be used to make sweeping indictments of all white people, and these generalizations have caused injuries to some white people who did not deserve them. Because of the spiritual rebirth which I was blessed to undergo as a result of my pilgrimage to the Holy City of Mecca, I no longer subscribe to sweeping indictments of one race."[9]

This reversal wasn't enough to change the course of those who despised X, though. On February 21, 1965, Malcolm X was assassinated while giving a speech on stage at the Audubon Ballroom in New York City. While three men were captured and convicted

6. Davies, *Malcolm X*, 98.
7. Haley and X, *Autobiography of Malcolm X*, 340.
8. X, *Malcolm X Speaks*, 32.
9. X, *Malcolm X Speaks*, 58.

for X's murder, there are many who adhere to a belief that "the official government version of how the assassination occurred is not credible," and that "the evidence points to government complicity in the murder."[10]

While we may never have an official answer as to the extent of the government's involvement with the murder of Malcolm X, one thing is certain: he represented a particular faction of the black community considered to be overwhelmingly dangerous to white power in the United States. And whether or not one agrees with X's militant ideas before the *hajj* versus after, it's clear that the worldly powers around him never afforded him the ability *to change*. After his pilgrimage to Mecca, X was a radically different individual with vastly different ideas about race, but that was all overshadowed by who he was in the past.

As Christians, the idea of leaving behind the old and embracing the new should be one we're deeply invested in. Our theological ideas of salvation, redemption, atonement, justification, and sanctification are all grounded in the belief that we can be freed from who we used to be and begin again. The message of the Christian faith is one that confesses that *we will all be changed*. Not only was X a prophetic voice in bringing awareness to the plight of black people in America, but he had experienced an existential transformation at the end of his life that only served to make him more open, more generous, and more inclusive. If that isn't the work of the Spirit in the life of a man deeply motivated by care for the oppressed, then I'm not sure what to call it.

REFLECT

1. At the beginning of this chapter, we saw a quotation from George Breitman which called X "one of the most misunderstood and misrepresented men of our time." Do you think this is true? Did your perspective on him change as you read?

---

10. Breitman et al., *Assassination of Malcolm X*, 7.

2. Even though Malcolm X wasn't a Christian, he was still deeply committed to his own religious tradition and—like many in this book—his faith was a driving factor in his activism on behalf of the black community. More than any other faith, Christianity shares a family tree with both Islam and Judaism thanks to their common ancestor, Abraham. How do you and/or your faith tradition make theological sense of these two other "Abrahamic" faiths?

3. For the bulk of his career before the *hajj*, X preached a message of liberation for the black community "by any means necessary." This would be a point of contention for many who criticized X for refusing to reject violence as a viable path of liberation (a topic we've touched on several times at this point in the book). In a way, X and MLK represent two sides of the spectrum for many people, with X representing violent revolution and MLK representing nonviolent revolution Do you feel like that's a fair characterization, especially considering X's shift in view later in life?

4. X shifted his thoughts regarding the white community after being exposed to people of different beliefs, convictions, and experiences. Can you recall a time this happened to you? What was it about that experience of exposure that was so revolutionary for you?

5. The Christian faith is all about change, both that which happens in the midst of this life and that which happens after death. Much like X, many of us go through seasons of change and transformation in our lives that leave us in a different place than before. How has your faith informed the way(s) you've changed over the course of your life? Have you found that, like for X, those seasons left you more compassionate and open to other people in the world around you?

Malcolm X

KEEP READING

Malcolm X

The Autobiography of Malcolm X. New York: Ballantine, 1992.
Malcolm X Speaks: Selected Speeches and Statements. Edited by George Breitman. New York: Grove Weidenfeld, 1990.

George Breitman; Herman Porter; and Baxter Smith

The Assassination of Malcolm X. New York: Pathfinder, 1976.

Clayborne Carson

Malcolm X: The FBI File. New York: Carroll & Graf, 1991.

John Henrick Clarke (editor)

Malcolm X: The Man and His Times. Trenton, NJ: Africa World, 1990.

Mark Davies

Malcolm X: Another Side of the Movement. New York: Silver Burdett, 1990.

Curtiss Paul Deyoung

"Malcolm X: 'Recognizing Every Human Being as a Human Being.'" In *Living Faith: How Faith Inspires Social Justice.* Minneapolis: Fortress, 2007.

Karl Evanzz

The Judas Factor: The Plot to Kill Malcolm X. New York: Thunder's Mouth, 1992.

Peter Goldman

The Death and Life of Malcolm X. Chicago: University of Illinois Press, 1979.

Manning Marable

Malcolm X: A Life of Reinvention. New York: Viking, 2011.

Les Payne and Tamara Payne

The Dead Are Arising: The Life of Malcolm X. New York: Liveright, 2020.

EXTREMISTS FOR LOVE

Joe Wood (editor)

Malcolm X: In Our Own Image. New York: St. Martin's, 1992.

14

William J. Barber II

In Caesar's world, where narcissistic leaders only cared about the grand and the greedy, the pompous and the pretentious, Jesus announces a revival led by and among the rejected. Caesar, who loved to put his face on money and buildings, Caesar, who catered to the greedy and led by fear and political shenanigans. Into Caesar's world—at that particular historical moment—Jesus announced prophetically that we are called to be a movement led by and with the poor.[1]

—WILLIAM J. BARBER II (1963–)

When he came to Nazareth, where he had been brought up, he went to the synagogue on the Sabbath day, as was his custom. He stood up to read, and the scroll of the prophet Isaiah was given to him. He unrolled the scroll and found the place where it was written: "The Spirit of the Lord is upon me, because he has anointed me to bring good news to the poor. He has sent me to proclaim the release to the captives and recovery of sight to the blind, to let the oppressed go free, to proclaim the year of the Lord's favor."

—LUKE 4:16–19

1. Barber, *We Are Called*, 12.

Extremists for Love

A QUESTION BEING ASKED more and more in the contemporary church is, what is the intersection between religious leadership and social leadership? Asked another way, to what extent should pastors also be activists? This is a question the Rev. Dr. William J. Barber II never had to ask. The son of a multi-vocational father who worked as a religious leader, high school teacher, and political organizer, Barber never found a Christianity-sans-justice to be an authentic expression of the faith. He recalls never having the modern experience of questioning God's existence like so many others, saying, "I cannot remember a time when I did not know God both to be real and to be about bringing justice in this world."[2]

A young child of the civil rights movement of the 1960s, Barber grew up under the influence of Martin Luther King Jr. and black prophetic Christianity. However, he'd also grown wary of the institutional church and its often-rigid unwillingness to get in "good trouble" (to use a term by John Lewis). As such, he attempted to avoid church ministry until he felt as if his calling had no other place to go: "It seemed as if I heard God's voice saying, 'Come out of the exile of false religion. Come out of the exile of the religion of idolatry and self-worship, which can only sustain oppression. Come out of the exile of religion that serves itself and avoids real people, the vulnerable people whom God adores.'"[3]

After pastoring a small congregation in Martinsville, Virginia, for three years following his seminary education, Barber returned to his native North Carolina and accepted a call to Greenleaf Christian Church in Goldsboro in 1993—a pastorate he would maintain for some thirty years until his retirement in 2023. It was this parish context that would nurture, not only Barber, but also the moral movement for which he was an architect. He would go on to build coalitions of people in Goldsboro and across the state to address issues of injustice—from education to housing to voting rights—eventually becoming the president of the North Carolina chapter of the National Association for the Advancement of Colored People (NAACP). However, the movements that would

2. Barber, *Third Reconstruction*, 6.
3. Barber, *Third Reconstruction*, 12–13.

rocket Barber to national recognition were still a few years from being born into the world.

In the late 2010s, North Carolina saw a seismic shift in the political makeup of its elected officials. After a decade of democratic control in the state house, senate, and governor's office, the chambers became increasingly red until Republicans controlled all three major components of the state government in 2013. Barber assesses the political landscape of the time like this: "In November 2012, with the help of an unconstitutional racially gerrymandered scheme in North Carolina, these forces hand-picked extremist candidates, slipped them thousands of dollars for their campaigns, and overwhelmed candidates who represented the interests of poor and working people."[4]

This new right-wing-controlled legislature enacted new policies and legislation that impacted the state's most vulnerable, including efforts to block the expansion of Medicaid, slash unemployment benefits and public education budgets, outlaw gay marriage, allow permitless carry of firearms, and intensely limit voting rights, among other things. A longtime state level organizer and coalition builder like Barber, though, already had the infrastructure in place for public resistance to such oppressive policies. Organizing a "people's assembly"—as opposed to the state's "general assembly"—on Monday, April 29, 2013, Barber and a group of others carried out an act of civil disobedience by occupying the gallery spaces inside the state capital building. During this protest, the group chanted, sang, and listened to speakers (Barber being one of them). That first day, seventeen people were arrested and taken to jail.

Following this event, Barber and his coalition elected to carry out another protest the following week, again on a Monday. At this one, thirty people were arrested. The following Monday, forty-nine people were arrested. These protests—dubbed "Moral Mondays"—continued through the months of June and July, leading to hundreds of arrests and thousands of North Carolinians being mobilized against unjust laws and policies. The Forward Together

---

4. Barber, *Forward Together*, 2.

Moral Movement, as it came to be known, had significantly disrupted the political atmosphere in North Carolina and the ripple effects were felt nationwide.

Out of the Forward Together movement came multiple new opportunities. First, "Repairers of the Breach" was established in 2014 as an educational initiative created by Barber and his coalition to equip leaders across the country with tools to organize against injustice in their respective contexts. Also, in 2017, the Poor People's Campaign was born—the leadership of which Barber shares with Rev. Dr. Liz Theoharis. It's a call to moral reformation in the United States and is committed to taking up MLK's vision for "a broad, fusion movement [to] unite poor and impacted communities across the country."[5] Most recently, however, Barber has retired from pastoral ministry and assumed a new role as professor and founding director of the Center for Public Theology and Public Policy at Yale Divinity School, embracing his calling as a teacher and preacher in a different way.

Now, given Barber's impressive résumé and list of credentials, he may serve (much like Cornel West) for some as a constant reminder that we haven't accomplished more with our lives. But it's worth pointing out that Barber's entire career and legacy stems from a single idea: that the God of the Bible is a God of liberation—an idea, it seems, that Jesus himself shared. When Jesus opened up the book of Isaiah and read out the prophecy that the day is coming when the prisoner will go free and good news will be brought to the poor—then claimed that it had, indeed, been fulfilled—he wasn't only speaking of his personal calling. He was providing a model for all future ministry carried out in his name. And in Jesus' historical context, it makes complete sense.

While we may not understand the ancient world's confusion of what we deem "political" and "religious," there was no such distinction in Jesus' Jewish tradition. The ancient Israelites' theological beliefs and legal system were one and the same. The fact that the God they worshiped was a God who liberated them from slavery in Egypt hung as a static reality over their day-to-day lives.

---

5. Poor People's Campaign, "National Call."

It dictated to them how the poor should be treated; how the earth should be treated; how the stranger should be treated. And when Jesus proclaimed the year of the Lord's favor, he wasn't envisioning a network of church revivals or worship services. No, he was envisioning a new reality in which there was no need, no injustice, no poverty, no lack; where all were in good health and cared for; where the powerful didn't relish in their privilege, but their responsibility. *This* is the reality Jesus envisioned, and the reality Barber's work anticipates.

REFLECT

1. Christianity has a long tradition of protest and civil disobedience against injustice. In a way, Jesus' death on the cross was an act of civil disobedience against the Roman Empire. Have you ever engaged in this kind of activism? Why or why not? If you have, where did you see God in that action?

2. Have you or someone you're close to been affected by laws—state or federal—that seem to have been targeted against poor and vulnerable populations? Who did you see advocating for you/them at that time?

3. What role do you think the church and church leaders should play in political activism? Should ministry remain exclusively within the local parish and nonprofit realm, or should political advocacy be a part of it?

4. Do you think it's possible for the gospel to be *political* without being *partisan*? If so, how does the church engage in political advocacy without devolving into mere partisan allegiance?

KEEP READING

Rev. Dr. William J. Barber II

Forward Together: A Moral Message for the Nation. St. Louis: Chalice, 2014.

Revive Us Again: Vision and Action in Moral Organizing. Boston: Beacon, 2018.
The Third Reconstruction: How a Moral Movement Is Overcoming the Politics of Division and Fear. Boston: Beacon, 2016.
We Are Called to Be a Movement. New York: Workman, 2020.

15

Coretta Scott King

What I was experiencing was nothing compared to the suffering of our Lord, Jesus Christ. Through his suffering, Christians were redeemed. Somehow, I knew that Martin's and my suffering would not be in vain—it was constructive suffering that would help bring down the walls of segregation. It was not happenstance, but meaningful suffering to help people, both black and white, reach a higher purpose. Jesus had been crucified, but in the end He triumphed. I encouraged myself to hold onto my faith that what I was going through was meaningful, too.[1]

—Coretta Scott King (1927–2006)

I consider that the sufferings of this present time are not worth comparing with the glory about to be revealed to us.... We know that the whole creation has been groaning in labor pains until now; and not only the creation, but we ourselves, who have the first fruits of the Spirit, groan inwardly while we wait for adoption, the redemption of our bodies.

—Romans 8:18, 22–23

1. Scott King, *My Life*, 107.

Extremists for Love

IN THE INTEREST OF full disclosure, you should know that I haven't done the research to necessarily back this up, but I imagine that if you were to walk up to most any random person on the street or in the grocery store and ask, "Who was Coretta Scott King?" the answer they might be able to give you—if they could give one at all—is that she was Martin Luther King Jr.'s wife. Now, this isn't necessarily an *incorrect* answer, but it's certainly an *incomplete* answer.

Despite the fact that women have long been defined exclusively by their relationship to men—which is problematic in and of itself—this answer reduces an incredible person who did incredible things down to a single aspect of an otherwise complex identity. Coretta Scott King wasn't only the wife of a famous civil rights activist. She *was* a civil rights activist, a human rights activist, an anti-war activist, a mother, a Christian, and a talented singer. She was a key leader who gave her life to the struggle for racial justice in America as much as her husband and others did. And in many ways, we remember Martin's life and legacy as favorably as we do because of Coretta's advocacy after his death.

And this complexity is one that she herself embraced. In her memoir, *My Life, My Love, My Legacy*—from which the quote at the top if this chapter is taken—she reflects on her life in the early 1960s, saying,

> While the sit-ins and protests were taking new forms, my life also was taking a new shape. . . . While I was happy to be Martin's wife and the mother of his children, I was more than a wife while he lived and more than a widow after he died. On the one hand, I was a copartner with him, married not only to him but to the movement. Yet, there was also a corner of life that belonged exclusively to me. More and more, I served as public speaker when Martin asked me to stand in for him at certain functions. I continued to perform, giving concerts to raise money for the movement, and I continued my role as a spokeswoman for the peace movement that I had begun through the Quaker groups in Antioch.[2]

2. Scott King, *My Life*, 96–97.

The "Antioch" she references here is Antioch College in Yellow Springs, Ohio. She attended Antioch on a scholarship and studied elementary education and vocal performance. It was here that Scott King became interested in activism and began to claim the title of "pacifist" in accordance with her understanding of the Christian faith: "it accorded with what I had been taught as a Christian: to love thy neighbor as thyself."[3] It was also here at Antioch that she began to become disenchanted with organized religion, eventually building relationships with Unitarians and Quakers.

After she left Antioch, she attended the New England Conservatory of Music in Boston; the place she would eventually be introduced to a young minister named Martin who was doing his PhD at Boston University. To hear Coretta tell it, as soon as she heard that "the young man was a minister I lost interest, for I began to think of the stereotypes of ministers I had known—fundamentalists in their thinking, very narrow, and overly pious."[4] All that being said, though, Martin must have broken with her stereotypes of the minister because they were married in June 1953, about a year and a half after they met.

Coretta would labor alongside Martin for the next fifteen years. Within that time, she not only supported the civil rights movement in the United States through speaking engagements, fundraising concerts, and being a strategic partner to Martin, but also used her voice and influence abroad as well. Most notably, she was invited to Geneva, Switzerland, by the Women's Strike for Peace as a delegate for talks regarding the ban of atomic weapons.[5] In his posthumously assembled autobiography, Martin recalls Coretta's personal fervor for this work: "My wife was always stronger than I was through the struggle. . . . She saw the greatness of the movement and had a unique willingness to sacrifice herself for its continuation."[6]

3. Scott King, *My Life*, 28.
4. Scott King, *My Life with Martin*, 50.
5. Scott King, *My Life with Martin*, 193.
6. King, *Autobiography*, 37.

Extremists for Love

It feels a bit dissonant to hear a man who would eventually be assassinated for his activism talking about his wife as the one who sacrificed herself for the civil rights movement. But, to put it bluntly, he was right. Coretta sacrificed her former dreams of being a professional musician for the cause of racial justice; she sacrificed opportunities in order to care for her children so Martin could travel and speak, and not to mention the fact that she also lost her partner in the process. The death of her husband didn't stop her from living into her calling, though. Four days after Martin's assassination on April 4, 1968, she was on the streets in Memphis supporting sanitation workers—the protest King was supposed to attend when he was shot on his hotel room balcony. The next day, Coretta and her four children laid Martin to rest.

Coretta continued to labor for the dream of a just and equitable society for the rest of her life, albeit without her husband at her side. She would advocate for the ending of the Vietnam War, helped organize workers and unions across several different fields, and aided in international peace efforts in South Africa, the USSR, and others. For good or for ill, though, what she might be most well-known for on this side of Martin's death is being "the architect of the King legacy."[7] She would go on to be the driving force behind the establishment of MLK's birthday as a national holiday, and established what is currently known as the Martin Luther King Jr. Center for Nonviolent Social Change, or The King Center, in Atlanta, Georgia. The Center was meant to be "not just a place, not just a building, but a spirit, one undergirded with his philosophy of nonviolence and love in action."[8]

Coretta Scott King stands as a towering figure of commitment, sacrifice, and persistence in the history of the black fight in America. And whereas many people couldn't see beyond Martin's leadership in the civil rights movement, Coretta had the courage to understand—in the face of overwhelming pain—that this movement was bigger than just one man. Despite the sufferings she endured, including the far-too-soon death of her husband, she

---

7. Scott King, *My Life*, 184.
8. Scott King, *My Life*, 186.

refused to be silenced or derailed. It was her belief in a beloved community marked by love, grace, and mercy that propelled, and continues to propel, the vision of nonviolent social change. Ultimately, she had *hope*; and it was this hope which allowed her to believe that, eventually, this beloved community can be a reality: "I believe future generations will have the courage, the love, and the faith to get this done. This is my hope, and this is my prayer."[9]

REFLECT

1. Think about the two quotations at the top of this chapter. Both talk about our current state of suffering and how, in some way, it has a role to play in redeeming an unjust present and building a better future. What do you think Coretta meant when she described her and Martin's sufferings as "constructive suffering that would help bring down the walls of segregation"? Do you think classifying suffering as "constructive" or "redemptive" might be problematic at times? Why or why not?

2. Coretta often got lost in her husband's shadow despite the fact that she was doing amazing work of her own, both for the civil rights movement at home and the wider movement for world peace abroad. Unfortunately, this isn't an uncommon reality for many women, especially in the Christian tradition. What do you believe the church's responsibility is, now and in the future, to tearing down the barriers that preclude women's full inclusion and leadership? How can we go about that in our local churches? Our social movements? Our governments?

3. Knowing that our current social and political reality is not conducive to full liberation and freedom of all people, Coretta placed her faith in the future generations of the world to "get this done." How can we in the church—especially those of us

---

9. Scott King, *My Life*, 330.

in positions of leadership—be encouraging and inspiring our young people to work towards justice? How might we be able to put that into practice in our preaching? Our small groups? Our mission trips?

KEEP READING

Coretta Scott King

My Life, My Love, My Legacy. New York: Henry Holt, 2017.
My Life with Martin Luther King, Jr. New York: Henry Holt, 1993.

16

Fannie Lou Hamer

So we are faced with a problem that is not flesh and blood, but we are facing principalities, and powers and spiritual wickedness in high places: that's what St. Paul told us. And that's what he meant. America created this problem. And we forgive America, even though we were brought here on the slave ships from Africa. Even though the dignity was taken away from the black men, and even though the black women had to bear not only their own kids, but kids for the white slave owners. We forgive America for that. But we're looking for this check now, that's long past due, to let us have our share in political and economic power, so that we can have a great country, together.[1]

—Fannie Lou Hamer (1917–1977)

Put on the whole armor of God, so that you may be able to stand against the wiles of the Devil. For our struggle is not against enemies of blood and flesh, but against the rulers, against the authorities, against the cosmic powers of this present darkness, against the spiritual forces of evil in the heavenly places.

—Ephesians 6:11–12

1. Hamer, "Sick and Tired," 180.

Extremists for Love

For good or for ill (depending on your chosen economic philosophy), our society has long pushed the good ol' pull-yourself-up-by-your-bootstraps American work ethic. And because of that, at least in part, it's no surprise that we absolutely love our underdog stories. Movies, music, books, television shows—our entire culture is full of the rags-to-riches, Cinderella-type tales of people "making it" after coming from nothing. To an extent, I think, we embrace these narratives because we want to find ourselves at the center of them one day. After all, America has no poor people, just "temporarily embarrassed capitalists."[2]

With all that being said, though, it's surprising that the figure of Fannie Lou Hamer isn't more popular in our national dialogue and storytelling. Born to a family of sharecroppers in 1917, Hamer was the youngest of twenty children—a family of fourteen boys and six girls—who grew up in post-Civil War Mississippi. And as one might expect, her family lived a life characterized by hardship and struggle: "Life was worse than hard. . . . It was *horrible*!" she once recalled.[3]

But as she was a black woman in the Jim Crow South with only about six years of formal education, opportunities for social mobility were scarce. Thus, her adult life mirrored that of the one she was accustomed to . . . at least for a while. In 1944, she married a fellow sharecropper named Perry (or "Pap") and continued working in the cotton fields of Mississippi for nearly another twenty years. In the early 1960s, though, Hamer decided that she could no longer sustain abuse and exploitation at the hands of white supremacists. This decision was influenced, in part, by an experience in a doctor's office.

In 1961, Hamer underwent surgery and when she awoke, she realized that she had, without consent, received a hysterectomy—a practice so common that it received its own nickname: a "Mississippi Appendectomy." As a brief aside: the forced sterilization of black women has, unfortunately, a long history in the United States and is just one example of the ways our country has perpetrated

---

2. Steinbeck, "Primer on the 30's," 93.
3. Asch, *Senator and the Sharecropper*, 53, emphasis original.

a campaign of eugenics over time. While I know this may sound fantastical and unrealistic to some, it has indeed been thoroughly documented.[4]

In any case, though, Hamer's involuntary hysterectomy wasn't her first experience with racial discrimination, and it certainly wouldn't be her last. In fact, her most prominent claim-to-fame wouldn't come until the years following when, in 1963, she attempted to register to vote. And according to her biographer, "once Fannie Lou Hamer tried to register to vote, there was no turning back to life on the plantation. Her course, and that of her husband, was irrevocably altered."[5] This attempt not only resulted in an altered life trajectory, but also caused the loss of her employment, eviction by her landlord, and her attempted murder. After returning to the registration office three times, however, Hamer was finally able to complete the paperwork (including a racist "literacy" test which required one to write an interpretation of the Mississippi State Constitution) and was one of the first African Americans in the state to register to vote.[6]

Given the ongoing and persistent toils that Hamer and her family had to deal with from childhood, one might wonder how she remained motivated to continue in this work. After all, one might argue that quietly carrying on a normal day-to-day and adhering to the status quo would be the safer and smarter option. Hamer didn't see it this way, though, due in large part to her faith: "Christ was a revolutionary person, out there where it was happening. That's what God is all about, and that's where I get my strength."[7]

Unfortunately, that strength would continue to be necessary. Hamer became an organizer in Mississippi and would start working with the Student Nonviolent Coordinating Committee (SNCC). Through this experience, and due to disillusionment

---

4. For more on American eugenics, see Black, *War against the Weak;* and Stern, *Eugenics Nation*.
5. Mills, *This Little Light*, 43.
6. Rubel, *Fannie Lou Hamer*, 68.
7. Bridges, *Resurrection Song*, 102.

with the current political parties, Hamer and others formed the Mississippi Freedom Democratic Party (MFDP) with the intention of unseating the all-white Mississippi delegation to the 1964 Democratic National Convention (DNC). Hamer would travel to the convention and give an impassioned, televised speech about the state of the black community in the South. While ultimately failing to unseat the delegates in 1964, the party succeeded four years later when, in 1968, Hamer and others unseated Mississippi's delegation to the DNC and received a standing ovation as they took their seats.

Hamer continued in public service on both the national and state levels until her death nine years later in 1977. While she carried on this work, she never lost faith, in either the democratic process or the God she had long believed in. Less than a year before her death, she attended a protest at the Mississippi state capitol building where she led a group in singing "This Little Light of Mine" in front of a statue commemorating Senator Theodore Bilbo: a white supremacist and segregationist. And if that weren't enough, her final interview—given only months before dying of cancer and heart failure—shows her ongoing commitment to the example of Christ as she remembered all those who risked their personal wellbeing for the cause: "Even when Christ hung on the cross, he said greater love has no man than the one who is willing to lay down his life for his friends. Even though they was [sic] aware they might die, they still came. These are the things we have to think about. These are the things we can't sweep under the rug. And these are the things that still give me hope."[8]

Fannie Lou Hamer's life was defined by struggle, be it physical, mental, emotional, or spiritual. From the injustice done to her body by a racist doctor, to the injustice she experienced at the polls as she attempted to exercise her constitutional right to vote, Hamer embodied the plight of the black community—and black women in particular—in her efforts to merely live a free and dignified life. Through all that struggle, though, she never lost hope. She remained committed to letting her light shine, and that light

8. Mills, *This Little Light of Mine*, 307.

made all the difference. It not only lit the way for her and all those around her to fight for the life that they were inherently entitled to, but it still continues to light that path today.

REFLECT

1. Hamer was someone who came from an impoverished background and was able to achieve a different kind of life. We often point to stories like these as examples that "anyone can make it." How might we reframe this story and think of it, not as a story of rags-to-riches, but as a story of exploitation-to-dignity? Why do you think it might be important to think about stories like these in a new light?

2. Part of Hamer's story was an insidious instance of healthcare injustice in the form of a "Mississippi Appendectomy," or unauthorized hysterectomy. Have you heard of things like this happening elsewhere? How do you think injustice could still be at work in the American healthcare system today?

3. Hamer refers to Christ as a "revolutionary person." Given Hamer's historical context, what passages of Scripture do you think might have led her to this conclusion? What parts of the gospels might have given her the impression of Jesus as a "revolutionary person"?

4. Whether it was related to registering to vote, attempting to unseat Mississippi's all-white delegation to the DNC, her chronic mistreatment at the hands of white people, or anything else, Hamer showcased what it means to "let your light shine"—a sentiment she attested to until the very end of her life. What might it mean to let *our* light shine today? How can we follow Hamer's example as individuals? As the church?

KEEP READING

Chris Myers Asch
The Senator and the Sharecropper: The Freedom Struggles of James O. Eastland and Fannie Lou Hamer. New York: New Press, 2008.

Kay Mills
This Little Light of Mine: The Life of Fannie Lou Hamer. New York: Dutton, 1993.

David Rubel
Fannie Lou Hamer: From Sharecropping to Politics. New York: Silver Burdett, 1990.

17

Ida B. Wells-Barnett

It is with no pleasure I have dipped my hands in the corruption here exposed. Somebody must show that the Afro-American race is more sinned against than sinning, and it seems to have fallen upon me to do so. The awful death-roll that Judge Lynch is calling every week is appalling, not only because of the lives it takes, the rank cruelty and outrage of the victims, but because of the prejudice it fosters and the stain it places against the good name of a weak race.[1]

—Ida B. Wells-Barnett (1862–1931)

The hour is coming, indeed it has come, when you will be scattered, each one to his home, and you will leave me alone. Yet I am not alone because the Father is with me. I have said this to you, so that in me you may have peace. In the world you face persecution. But take courage; I have conquered the world!

—John 16:32–33

---

1. Wells-Barnett, "Southern Horrors," 14–15.

"ETERNAL VIGILANCE IS THE price of liberty."[2] This is how Wells-Barnett began the last chapter of her autobiography; a text which would remain unfinished upon her death in 1931. And "eternal vigilance" is certainly a term with which she is easily associated. Even in death, her legacy continues to inspire, challenge, and influence the dialogue around race in America (whether we know it or not).

Wells-Barnett was born into the tempestuous Civil War-era as a slave in 1862—a mere six months before the Emancipation Proclamation would take effect in January 1863 and free African Americans from the plight of chattel slavery (though this process of emancipation wasn't immediate and had clear difficulties as the war raged on for another two years). While the end of the Civil War in 1865 may have brought some reprieve for the family, it was short lived. Not only was there consistent and ongoing racial violence across the South, but in 1878, when Wells-Barnett was only sixteen years old (the oldest of her family's eight children), an epidemic struck the Mississippi town in which she lived, resulting in the death of both her parents, as well as her youngest brother. These deaths were bookended by the deaths of two of her other siblings—one before the epidemic and one after. Thus, as a teenager, Wells-Barnett was thrust into the position of caring for her remaining brothers and sisters, which she did. Becoming a teacher, she relocated with her two young sisters to Tennessee, about five years after the epidemic, to pursue a teaching opportunity in Memphis, and it was here that Wells-Barnett would begin her career of fighting against injustice.

After being told by a train conductor that she wasn't allowed to ride in any of the nonsmoking cars, she proceeded to sue the railroad for not providing a "separate, *but equal*" alternative to the regular train car she desired to ride in. She would go on to win her case, but a short six months later, the Tennessee Supreme Court would reverse the decision; an event which prompted this reflection in her diary: "O God, is there no redress, no peace, no justice in this land for us? Thou hast always fought the battles of the weak

---

2. Wells-Barnett, *Crusade for Justice*, 415.

and oppressed. Come to my aid at this moment and teach me what to do, for I am sorely, bitterly disappointed. Show us the way, even as Thou led the children of Israel out of bondage into the promised land."[3]

Her diary wasn't the only place where Wells-Barnett would voice her concerns and frustrations, though. She wrote occasionally for various black newspapers and publications, registering her opinions on the local happenings of the day. These opportunities eventually led to an editorship with the *Free Speech and Headlight*—a publication born out of a merger of two separate black papers. She became a part owner of the paper and, "with Wells as editor, the paper trumpeted her conviction that African Americans should not meekly settle for white domination."[4]

Following the unjust killing of a good friend at the hands of the white community, Wells-Barnett used her newfound platform to take aim at one particular practice: lynching. A long-standing method of extrajudicial execution in the United States, lynching became racialized in the post-Civil War era as a new way to terrorize blacks in the absence of slavery's institution. While official records often indicate the lynching of black people (especially black men) as the resultant punishment for crimes such as rape or theft, Wells-Barnett began using her journalistic skills to prove these narratives as bogus, push back against incorrect assumptions, and reeducate people about the abhorrent practice.

Rather than lynching being the practice of poor, uneducated whites, Wells-Barnett showed that these acts were carried out at the direction of "leading business men, in the leading business center";[5] she exposed the inconsistency and hypocrisy of miscegenation laws and the one-sided ways they were used to discourage interracial sex, showcasing how white men weren't punished for having relations with black women, but black men were lynched if they had relations with white women; she laid plain the fact that

---

3. Duster, "Introduction," xvii. See also McMurry, *To Keep the Waters*, 68–75.

4. Davidson, *"They Say,"* 114.

5. McMurry, *To Keep the Waters*, 157.

rape—the accusation often used by white mobs to justify a black lynching—was only a concern when the alleged victim was a white woman, but was not a concern when it came to the rape of black women. And Wells-Barnett did all this in the face of widespread, societal fear of speaking out against lynching. She assessed the hesitancy to accurately cover the topic of lynching like this: "This cry has had its effect. It has closed the heart, stifled the conscience, warped the judgment and hushed the voice of press and pulpit on the subject of lynch law throughout this 'land of liberty.' Men who stand high in the esteem of the public . . . stand as cowards who fear to open their mouths before this great outrage."[6]

The fear that Wells-Barnett speaks of is not misplaced. Her extensive coverage and criticism of lynching led to her press at the *Free Speech* being destroyed by a white mob, along with death threats against her life. As word of these happenings spread across the globe, she was invited to come and lecture on lynching in Britain, where she implored listening ears abroad to do what seemed impossible on the home front: "It is because of the moral cowardice shown by the Christian bodies of my own country . . . that I come to England and ask them to do what Unitarian along with other Christian bodies in America have failed to do—speak out against this great evil . . . and put a stop to it."[7]

Unfortunately, Wells-Barnett didn't see the end of lynching in her lifetime. Her impact on the cause, however, was undeniable. She would go on to play a key role in the formation of several organizations who would carry on her work, not the least of which being the National Association for the Advancement of Colored People (NAACP) and the National Association of Colored Women (NACW), and her legacy would serve as an enduring inspiration to those who sought the liberation of black people from oppression and persecution in America, particularly in the form of extra-judicial execution via lynching. And in our contemporary post-Ferguson context, where the Black Lives Matter movement

---

6. Wells-Barnett, "Southern Horrors," 30.
7. Silkey, *Black Woman Reformer*, 101.

is front and center, her legacy has been launched back into the national dialogue.

In a 2017 *Washington Post* article, Brown University professor Keisha Blain notes that "today, black Americans die at the hands of police at a rate that is almost equivalent to the number of documented lynchings during the early 20th century."[8] Long considered a modern manifestation of the nineteenth- and twentieth-century lynching tradition, the killing of unarmed black people at the hands of law enforcement in contemporary America has become the same rallying point that lynching was for Wells-Barnett over a hundred years ago. And while we can't dismiss the usefulness of protests, events of civil disobedience, and calls for accountability, the solution (Blain proposes) is the same one Wells-Barnett proposed to end lynching: establish federal, legal protections for black lives. While the "Emmett Till Antilynching Act" was signed into law in 2022, making lynching a federal hate crime and realizing Wells-Barnett's dream a century after the fact, we still must deal with the fact that the sentiment and logic of lynching still remains, albeit in an altered state.

After all Wells-Barnett experienced in her lifetime of advocacy and justice work, she was no stranger to the reality of what Jesus refers to as "the world" in John 16. In that world, where darkness seems to saturate people's lives, people like Ida B. Wells-Barnett are the light. The reality that Jesus prophesied by claiming he had overcome the world is the same one that Wells-Barnett invested her life in bringing to fruition. While persecution existed, and continues to exist today, she was sure that the day was coming when the world would no longer hold power over the lives of black people and that we all have a role to play in ensuring a future of dignity and self-determination for those communities who currently lack them.

---

8. Blain, "Ida B. Wells."

REFLECT

1. Do you remember the first time you saw a historical photograph of a lynching? How did it make you feel? Angry? Scared? Sad?

2. Lynchings used to be considered almost social events for white communities who would often bring children along and pose for pictures next to the murdered black bodies. Why do you think a lot of people who lived during the lynching era didn't have the same kind of visceral reaction to the practice that we have today?

3. Wells-Barnett, like many of the individuals we're talking about in this book, spoke out against racial injustice at great personal risk and sustained regular threats against her life as a result. In your opinion, do we have a responsibility to speak out against such injustice today even if it might put us in harm's way? Why or why not?

4. Wells-Barnett's primary mode of resistance against lynching was her career as a journalist, as someone who could expose the facts of a case and discredit bogus, racist claims. In our current political climate, which continues to be saturated with Trumpian accusations of "fake news," how important do you think good, honest journalism is to the work of social and racial justice?

KEEP READING

Ida B. Wells-Barnett

Crusade for Justice: The Autobiography of Ida B. Wells. Chicago: University of Chicago Press, 1970.

Selected Works of Ida B. Wells-Barnett. Edited by Trudier Harris. New York: Oxford University Press, 1991.

Ida B. Wells-Barnett

James West Davidson

"They Say": Ida B. Wells and the Reconstruction of Race. New York: Oxford University Press, 2007.

Linda O. McMurry

To Keep the Waters Troubled: The Life of Ida B. Wells. New York: Oxford University Press, 1998.

Angela Shelf Medearis

Princess of the Press: The Story of Ida B. Wells-Barnett. New York: Lodestar, 1997.

Ruth A. Rouff

Ida B. Wells: A Woman of Courage. West Berlin, NJ: Townsend, 2010.

Sarah L. Silkey

Black Woman Reformer: Ida B. Wells, Lynching, and Transatlantic Activism. Athens: University of Georgia Press, 2015.

Catherine A. Welch

Ida B. Wells-Barnett: Powerhouse with a Pen. Minneapolis: Carolrhoda, 2000.

18

Colin Kaepernick

I am not looking for approval. I have to stand up for people that are oppressed.... If they take football away, my endorsements from me, I know that I stood up for what is right.[1]

—Colin Kaepernick (1987–)

Though an army encamp against me, my heart shall not fear; though war rise up against me, yet I will be confident.

—Psalm 27:3

It's not lost on me that some readers may have turned the page over to this chapter and let out a "Huh?" of confusion. In a book that, so far, has been largely about abolitionists, theologians, political figures, and pastors, why are we talking about a former NFL quarterback who hasn't seen the field in the better part of a decade? And while that reaction makes sense on the surface, we need not look far to realize the long history of professional athletes publicly speaking out against injustice.

Jesse Owens made a statement by participating in the 1936 Olympic games—overseen by none other than Adolf Hitler—and

1. Wyche, "Colin Kaepernick."

subsequently winning four gold medals against the German nation whose goal it was to showcase the phenomenon of Aryan supremacy. Jackie Robinson became a household name as the first black athlete to play in Major League Baseball. World heavyweight boxing champion Muhammad Ali famously refused to submit to the United States draft during the Vietnam War, and was publicly supported by NBA star Bill Russell, a civil rights activist in his own right. Few images are more well known, however, than the photographs of John Carlos and Tommie Smith at the 1968 Mexico City Olympics, each raising a fist on the podium of the medal ceremony—an unambiguous endorsement of black power and the civil rights battle being waged on the home front.

All of these (and others) were the early forerunners of Colin Kaepernick, the San Francisco 49ers quarterback who, in 2016, rebelliously refused to stand during the pre-game national anthem in protest of police brutality. Initially sitting during the anthem, Kaepernick was eventually persuaded by teammate Eric Reid and veteran-turned-NFL long-snapper Nate Boyer to take a knee instead in an effort to thread the needle of protesting black oppression while also showing respect for military members. *Sports Illustrated* even published a story on this exact dilemma shortly after Kaepernick's actions were launched into the national dialogue: "The very reason the criticism that Kaepernick 'disrespected the troops' is unfair is because his critics are projecting what the national anthem means to *them*. There is no objective meaning of the anthem, and Kaepernick is perfectly legitimate in protesting what it means to him."[2]

Kaepernick's protest came on the heels of the Ferguson Uprising, the formation of Black Lives Matter, and the notable killings of Freddie Gray in Baltimore, Alton Sterling in Baton Rouge, and Philando Castile in Minneapolis—the families of whom all received multi-million-dollar wrongful death lawsuit settlements from their respective cities, but never saw any of their loved ones' killers convicted of a crime. When asked by the media about his refusal to stand for the anthem, Kaepernick responded, "I am not

2. Jacobs, "Week Under Review."

going to stand up to show pride in a flag for a country that oppresses black people and people of color.... To me, this is bigger than football and it would be selfish on my part to look the other way. There are bodies in the street and people getting paid leave and getting away with murder."[3] And his symbolic actions didn't remain exclusive to him; they spread. Shortly after he first took a knee, other players at the professional, collegiate, and high school levels all followed suit, mirroring Kaepernick's posture during the national anthem prior to their own events.

While Kaepernick's actions drew criticism from many in the football community and general public—ultimately (some speculate, and this author is inclined to agree) costing him his career in professional football, as he went unsigned by any NFL team in the 2017 season—his protest didn't emerge in a vacuum. In addition to the long line of athletes-of-conscience mentioned above, Kaepernick's kneeling is especially reminiscent of the Civil Rights era's tradition of nonviolence and civil disobedience. He's not being violent or engaging in vindictive acts of retribution; he's peacefully kneeling before a football game. The fact that this simple act has vexed so many in the American public, especially Christians and churchgoing folk, should be telling for us.

Rev. Angela Denker says as much in her *Washington Post* article about Kaepernick: "This is about a deep fear of what Kaepernick has tapped into: a shaking of America's Christian roots and a question about who owns the narrative of Jesus: white evangelical Christian culture or African American liberation movements?"[4] While some may quibble over Denker's framing here in defense of Christ's "universality," we need to remember that theological claims and political claims aren't the same. While we can defend a *theological* claim that the narrative of Jesus belongs to everyone, we can't ignore the current social realities which expose the exact question Denker is forcing us to confront. White evangelical Christian culture and African American liberation movements are, historically, misaligned with one another. One is primarily

3. Wyche, "Colin Kaepernick."
4. Denker, "Colin Kaepernick."

interested in the inner life of religious piety while the other is primarily interested in piety's promise for liberation. One was inherited from generations of white colonialists and the other was inherited from generations of slaves and oppressed communities.

As white evangelicalism has much to learn and glean from the history of black Christianity in America, Kaepernick may just provide a place to start. After all, kneeling during the national anthem isn't really about the national anthem at all. It's about openly declaring the incompatibility between the way things are and the way they should be. It's easy to feel paralyzed and impotent by issues like racial injustice; systemic and resilient, we're prone to stare down the multi-headed hydra and rhetorically ask, "Well, what exactly am I supposed to do about this? I'm not a politician or an activist or a changemaker. I'm just [fill-in-the-blank]." But in figures like Kaepernick, we're offered an answer about what we're supposed to do: *whatever we're able*. Kaepernick was just a professional athlete, but he used what he was able—an audience and a platform—to shed light on black oppression.

While it will look different for all of us depending on where we live, what we do for work, how our families are structured, etc. taking a public stand against injustice, racism, police brutality, and empire should be the absolute minimum we expect of ourselves. Kaepernick, like a modern prophet calling out to us from the wilderness, has modeled for us what it looks like to do as much amidst the cultural wars raging around us. And if we can do that— if we can remain confident and steadfast in our convictions, even when they're unpopular—then we can begin the real work of taking steps toward actually effecting change.

REFLECT

1. If you have memory of former generations of athletes who used their platforms to bring light to issues of racial (or other) injustice, how do you remember the social reception of those acts? How was the political climate different in those

times? Was there widespread outrage, like with Kaepernick's kneeling during the national anthem, or did people react differently?

2. The outrage over Kaepernick's protest has exposed to us a kind of "confusion" of Christianity and nationalism: tying love of God and love of country so closely together that to criticize America is essentially to criticize God. Where in your own church or ministry have you seen this same kind of confusion of Christianity and nationalism?

3. One of the articles quoted above talks about who "owns" the narrative of Jesus. It's common knowledge that Jesus has been leveraged by many people across history for both oppressive and liberating aims. In our current American society, who do you feel "owns" the Jesus narrative currently? How do you see it being utilized to both perpetrate injustice and fight injustice in your context?

4. Kaepernick is a contemporary model of what it looks like to use one's platform to stand against oppression regardless of consequences. What steps might you/your church/your church's leadership take to embrace this same courageous mentality and be willing to pay the costs of doing what's right?

KEEP READING

Cem Abanazir

Political Expression in Sports: Transnational Challenges, Moral Defences. New York: Routledge, 2023.

Dave Zirin

The Kaepernick Effect: Taking a Knee, Changing the World. New York: New Press, 2021.

19

Michelle Alexander

It is far more convenient to imagine that a majority of young African American men in urban areas freely chose a life of crime than to accept the real possibility that their lives were structured in a way that virtually guaranteed their early admission into a system from which they can never escape. Most people are willing to acknowledge the existence of the cage but insist that a door has been left open.[1]

—Michelle Alexander (1967–)

The spirit of the Lord God is upon me, because the Lord has anointed me; he has sent me to bring good news to the oppressed, to bind up the brokenhearted, to proclaim liberty to the captives, and release to the prisoners; to proclaim the year of the Lord's favor, and the day of vengeance of our God; to comfort all who mourn; to provide for those who mourn in Zion—to give them a garland instead of ashes, the oil of gladness instead of mourning, the mantle of praise instead of a faint spirit. They will be called oaks of righteousness, the planting of the Lord, to display his glory.

—Isaiah 61:1–3

1. Alexander, *New Jim Crow*, 184–85.

Extremists for Love

REMEMBER ALL THE WAY back to the very first chapter of this book when I mentioned the course I took in college called "Race, Rights, and Religion after Ferguson"? And how, after critically engaging with figures like Martin Luther King Jr. and Malcolm X for the very first time, the scales began to fall from my eyes and I finally began to see the reality of systemic racism in the United States? Well, it was also during that same class that I was introduced to the work of Michelle Alexander (in case you couldn't tell, it was an impactful semester for me).

Alexander is a lawyer, scholar, and writer who has held prestigious academic appointments at Stanford, Ohio State University, and (somewhat recently) Union Theological Seminary as a visiting professor. Her book, *The New Jim Crow: Mass Incarceration in an Age of Colorblindness*, proved a groundbreaking text upon its first printing in 2010. In its pages, she lays out a forceful argument that (contrary to many people's beliefs) "we have not ended racial caste in America; we have merely redesigned it."[2]

Alexander examines the history of racial discrimination in the United States, walking through slavery, the Civil War, Reconstruction, Jim Crow laws, the Civil Rights movement, and into modernity. Through this process, she maintains a grasp on the thread of language, ideas, and concepts about race, and how they've been continually rehashed and repackaged throughout time to be less and less explicit, but no less present. For example, she discusses how, in the 1970s and 1980s, "conservatives gave lip service to the goal of racial equality but actively resisted desegregation, busing, and civil rights enforcement," how welfare was indirectly framed "as a contest between hardworking, blue-collar whites and poor blacks who refused to work," and how Ronald Reagan carried on the work of previous conservatives in "develop[ing] a strategy of exploiting racial hostility or resentment for political gain without making explicit reference to race."[3]

This all comes to a head in the contemporary world, however, in the War on Drugs—another effort "cloaked in race-neutral

---

2. Alexander, *New Jim Crow*, 2.
3. Alexander, *New Jim Crow*, 47–48.

language."[4] This "war," Alexander contends has much less to do with keeping communities safe by way of eliminating dangerous substances and much more to do with a targeted attack on people of color. And before anyone jumps to the conclusion that drug use is more prevalent in communities of color versus white communities, there is data to back up Alexander's argument. Here, it is worth quoting Alexander at length:

> One study, for example, published in 2000 by the National Institute on Drug Abuse reported that white students use cocaine at seven times the rate of black students, and use heroine at seven times the rate of black students. That same survey revealed that nearly identical percentages of white and black high school seniors use marijuana. The National Household Survey on Drug Abuse reported in 2000 that white youth aged 12–17 are more than a third more likely to have sold illegal drugs than African American youth. Thus the very same year, Human Rights Watch was reporting that African Americans were being arrested and imprisoned at unprecedented rates, government data revealed that blacks were more likely to be guilty of drug crimes than whites.[5]

This all exists against a backdrop of racial disparity in arrests and convictions of blacks over whites. According to the ACLU, "Black people in the United States are incarcerated in state prisons at nearly five times the rate of white Americans" and "nationally, one in 81 Black adults in the US is serving time in state prison."[6]

And while some might assume that people who produce research like this have some kind of inherent disposition toward "progressive" stances on social issues, Alexander is quick to acknowledge that the central premise of her book was one she arrived at reluctantly: "Ten years ago, I would have argued strenuously against the central claim made here. . . . Never did I seriously consider the possibility that a new racial caste system was

---

4. Alexander, *New Jim Crow*, 54.
5. Alexander, *New Jim Crow*, 99.
6. American Civil Liberties Union, "Race and Criminal Justice."

operating in this country. The new system had been developed and implemented swiftly, and was largely invisible, even to people, like me, who spent most of their waking hours fighting for justice."[7] However, she eventually began to shift her perspective and acknowledge that she might have been wrong.

It was this realization that led to her writing *The New Jim Crow*—a task which, while daunting and exhausting, she says was spurred on by the divine: "I must admit that, after a while, I tried to quit writing the book. Writing it was so much more difficult than I had imagined; I started to think it wasn't worth the effort. But the Spirit was working in my life in ways that I did not fully understand."[8] The Spirit at work in Alexander's analysis of the criminal justice system is the same Spirit who was at work in me all those years ago as I began to understand that the criminal justice system isn't broken, but that it's functioning *exactly* as it was designed. Our current system of the disproportionate arrests, convictions, and mass incarceration of black bodies in the United States is the result of America's original sin evolving; a living, breathing shadow which has continued to adapt to every new instance of liberation and justice breaking forth.

If we truly believe that the God we proclaim from our pulpits is the same God who broke the chains of slavery (both in Egypt and the Antebellum South) and who proclaims a message of liberty and freedom to captives and prisoners, then we *must* believe that our faith has something to say about the new Jim Crow. Alexander's work, for myself and many, has functioned like a tiny pinprick of Paul's vision on the road to Damascus: at once blinding and revelatory, leaving one no other option than to follow an altered path. As it says at the top of this chapter, many people believe a door remains open for African Americans to escape the cage of our current criminal justice system, but Alexander's work shows us that it's not that simple. Perhaps our role—as followers of Christ within whom the Spirit of the Lord is also at work—isn't so much to open the door to the cage, but to demolish the cage altogether.

7. Alexander, *New Jim Crow*, 2–3.
8. Alexander, "When the Spirit Says."

REFLECT

1. The central premise of Alexander's work is that racial caste in America has not been eliminated, but has evolved into a new form, incarnating in the criminal justice system. What do you think about the racial disparities in arrests and incarcerations? Do you believe this system is truly fair and balanced, or shows preference to one race over another?

2. In *The New Jim Crow*, Alexander talks about the elimination of race-based language in our public discourse, not as a tool of racial justice, but as a way for racism to move "underground" and become harder to detect. How do you see racism still at play in our society, albeit without explicitly racial language?

3. The Isa 61 passage above is well-known, not necessarily in its original context, but because Jesus quotes it in Luke 4 when he reads from a scroll in a synagogue. While both Isa 61 and Luke 4 have their own historical locations which inform how they should be interpreted, how do you think they can inform our ideas about Christianity today?

4. Both Alexander's work and this chapter's Scripture passage talk about "liberty to the captives" and "release to the prisoners." While, taken literally, this may seem implausible, how might the church be able to advocate for dignity, respect, and actual restoration to those subject to the criminal justice system?

KEEP READING

Michelle Alexander

The New Jim Crow: Mass Incarceration in an Age of Colorblindness. New York: New Press, 2011.

Derrick Bell

Faces at the Bottom of the Well: The Permanence of Racism. New York: Basic Books, 2018.

Isabel Wilkerson

Caste: The Origins of Our Discontent. New York: Random House, 2023.

20

The Black Lives Matter Movement

No amount of pants raising, voting, education, or removing hoodies would change the fact that a child was murdered by an adult who got away with it. Because in America, Black people are criminals whether we're eight years old or eighty years old, whether we have on a suit and tie . . . or whether we sag our pants, whether we have a PhD or GED or no degree at all. In America and around the world, Black lives did not matter.[1]

—ALICIA GARZA (1981–)

You stiff-necked people, uncircumcised in heart and ears, you are forever opposing the Holy Spirit, just as your ancestors used to do. Which of the prophets did your ancestors not persecute? They killed those who foretold the coming of the Righteous One, and now you have become his betrayers and murderers. You are the ones that received the law as ordained by angels, and yet you have not kept it.

—ACTS 7:51–53

---

1. Garza, *Purpose of Power*, 116.

Extremists for Love

IF YOU TAKE A trip through Ferguson, Missouri, and turn onto Canfield Drive, you'll enter an apartment community much like any other you've seen: large swaths of green grass stretching between buildings, children riding bikes, people on their small walk-out decks chatting with neighbors or driving by on their way to work. After a few minutes, though, you'll come upon a large, rectangular block of asphalt in the middle of the street that appears quite a bit newer than the rest of the road. While roadwork and infrastructure updates are as common in St. Louis as they are in any other major city, you might assume it was the result of public works carrying out repairs or something of the like.

That's not the case, though. The large, carved out area is, rather, the place where Michael Brown was shot six times and killed by police officer Darren Wilson in 2014, igniting a year's worth of protests and riots that drew national attention. In a way, the scarred asphalt of Canfield Drive—while easily overlooked by the outsider—stands not only as a constant reminder to the community's black residents of what happened to Brown and the fact that his killer walks free but also what could happen to them at the hands of law enforcement without repercussion. While Brown's killing had a galvanizing effect on the movement for black lives in the modern era, it was already on the forefront of people's minds.

Brown's death came just two years after the fatal shooting of Trayvon Martin in Florida at the hands of a gun-toting neighborhood watchman. The young Martin, armed with nothing but a bag of candy and a can of iced tea, was killed by George Zimmerman who was later acquitted of murder and manslaughter charges. It was between these two events in which young, black, unarmed, high school-aged boys were gunned down out of "self-defense" that the #BlackLivesMatter hashtag first emerged.

Now a full-blown international movement with dozens of chapters and over $8 million in funding, Black Lives Matter started as nothing more than a social media post by Alicia Garza, an activist and community organizer. In reaction to Zimmerman's acquittal, Garza expressed lament and rage at the lack of value assigned to black life in America: "Young black boys in this country are not safe. Black men in this country are not safe. This verdict will create many more George Zimmermans."[2] In the days and weeks that followed the message exploded, saturating all forms of social media under the guidance of Garza, Patrisse Cullors, and Opal Tometi—the three women who would lead the movement into the global organization it is today.

The message that Black Lives Matter wasn't without its critics, though. It didn't take long for an opposing faction to start spreading a similar, yet vastly different, message: *all* lives matter. While taken at face value, and outside the context of the patterned deaths of unarmed black people in the United States, such a statement seems relatively obvious and uncontroversial. When taken as a protest against the statement that Black Lives Matter, however, it assumes a different meaning. Having become a watchword of right-wing American politics (and being used by some on the left, such as Hillary Clinton), "all lives matter" has been embraced by politicians, celebrities, and pop culture figures who misunderstood "Black Lives Matter" as an exclusive statement; that black lives actually matter to the *exclusion* of all other lives.

However, this rationale is easily deflated. UC Berkeley professor Judith Butler debunks the exclusion argument in an interview with *The New York Times*: "If we jump too quickly to the universal formulation, 'all lives matter,' then we miss the fact that black people have not yet been included in the idea of 'all lives.'"[3] All over social media, others have made the comparison to a burning house, asking what would happen if the fire department showed up and refused to put the fire out, claiming, "all houses matter." Or going to the doctor with a broken arm or leg and your doctor refusing to treat it because "all bones matter." The question isn't whether or not all lives matter; the question is why, if all lives matter, do black lives continue to be taken as if they don't?

The underlying fear in refusing to affirm that Black Lives Matter is the fear that whiteness might no longer occupy the center of our racial conceptions. As such, there's a backlash against any

---

2. Garza, *Purpose of Power*, 110.
3. Yancy and Butler, "What's Wrong."

attempt to showcase black lives as equal with white ones. Garza says it well when she says that "change does not occur without backlash—at least, any change worth having—and that backlash is an indicator that the change is so powerful that the opposing forces resist that change with everything they have."[4]

This kind of backlash that the Black Lives Matter movement has experienced since its inception is nothing new to groups and organizations who speak truth to power and challenge the status quo. After all, this was the reality of the early church when it began to spread a radical message of love that lifted the oppressed, healed the sick, and embraced the outcast. As is mentioned above in the book of Acts, the Bible is full of stories of prophets being killed, the righteous being persecuted, and the powerful lashing out against the powerless who try to secure justice and dignity for themselves. The Black Lives Matter movement is, in a very real way, a prophetic movement in line with the movement Jesus started all that time ago.

For far too long, though, the church has been unwilling to boldly declare that Black Lives Matter because of the potential ramifications it might have on finances and membership. The question we must begin asking ourselves as we continue to minister to our communities and our world is, "what would it look like for *us* to preach and proclaim and affirm that Black Lives Matter?" And not merely in a well-crafted statement or a random Sunday morning mention, but in everything it does. The kingdom of God that Jesus talked so much about, that we spend so much time praying for and working on behalf of, is a kingdom in which Black Lives Matter.

We *must* begin believing that the only possible future is one in which Black Lives Matter and that it's to this future that the Holy Spirit is leading us. The stiff-necked people Stephen talks about in Acts 7 are the people who weren't willing to follow the Spirit; weren't willing to listen to the prophets; weren't willing to say the things that needed to be said and do the things that needed to be done. Either we can join their ranks and resist the liberating

---

4. Garza, "2014–2019," 382.

movement of the Spirit leading us to create a better world, or we can become extremists for love, agents of change, and have a hand in ushering in the kingdom where all lives can finally matter *precisely because* Black Lives Matter. The choice is ours.

REFLECT

1. What do you remember from the mid-2010s and the events that fostered the Black Lives Matter movement? What were your thoughts and feelings about what happened to Trayvon Martin and the Ferguson Uprising over the killing of Michael Brown? Have those feelings changed at all?

2. Black Lives Matter has continued to be a relevant message in the years since Martin and Brown, especially after the police-related deaths of George Floyd, Breonna Taylor, and Tyre Nichols. Did the events of 2012–2014 affect the way you responded to these more recent manifestations of police brutality? How did the video footage of both Floyd's and Nichols's deaths affect the way you approached the idea that Black Lives Matter less in this country than other lives?

3. The contention surrounding the "all lives matter" claim amid the barrage of black deaths in the US is a perfect example of why context matters. Why do you think it could be insensitive to respond to the claim that Black Lives Matter in this way?

4. This chapter ends with a challenge to the church to embrace the message that Black Lives Matter in all that it does. What ways might your church and/or ministry do this? What changes could be made to the mission and vision to take this claim seriously?

KEEP READING

Patrisse Cullors and Asha Bandele

When They Call You a Terrorist: A Black Lives Matter Memoir. New York: St. Martin's, 2017.

Patrisse Cullors

An Abolitionist's Handbook: 12 Steps to Changing Yourself and the World. New York: St. Martin's, 2021.

Kelly Brown Douglas

Resurrection Hope: A Future Where Black Lives Matter. Maryknoll, NY: Orbis, 2021.

Stand Your Ground: Black Bodies and the Justice of God. Maryknoll, NY: Orbis, 2015.

Leah Gunning Francis

Faith after Ferguson: Resilient Leadership in Pursuit of Racial Justice. St. Louis: Chalice, 2021.

Alicia Garza

The Purpose of Power: How We Come Together When We Fall Apart. New York: One World, 2020.

Angela N. Parker

If God Still Breathes, Why Can't I? Black Lives Matter and Biblical Authority. Grand Rapids: Eerdmans, 2021.

Epilogue

W. E. B. DuBois; Pauli Murray; Frederick Douglass Thurgood Marshall; Rosa Parks; Ruby Bridges; Jackie Robinson; Langston Hughes; Billie Holiday; Muhammad Ali; Bayard Rustin; Kelly Brown Douglas; Adam Clayton Powell Sr.; Bryan Stevenson; Gary Dorrien; Cedric Robinson; Ibram X. Kendi, Shirley Chisolm— These are some of the individuals I considered including in this volume who were ultimately left unexamined. As most writers would tell you, though, writing by its very nature requires difficult choices to be made, fiction and nonfiction alike. And in a book like this, which attempts to provide a primer of the people, groups, and ideas that have shaped the movement for racial justice in America, there is an endless number of courageous people who could have filled this book hundreds of times over.

All that being said, this book isn't a place to finish the conversation, but merely to begin it. Even though you may have worked hard to carve out time and intentionally reflect on what each chapter means for you, I implore you: DO NOT stop here. As I hope you've been able to see by now, racism is a pernicious shape-shifter with the ability to rearrange and change in any given time and space. However, those of us who have eyes to see and ears to hear find ourselves perpetually surrounded by its cacophony.

The whole point of this book is to help people develop the sight and hearing necessary to identify racism when and where it rears its ugly head. And that can be uncomfortable, especially in the church where we've often been taught to keep the world at arms' length. But if we're truly to be Christians—"little Christs"—then we can't ignore the fact that *God* didn't keep the world at arms' length. Instead, God became inextricably intertwined with it; being born in it and living in it and dying in it. As Christians, we're called to do the same. We're not here to separate ourselves and wait for some metaphysical end times to come and solve all our problems. No, we're called to both love God *and* neighbor. And much of the time, that means doing the hard work of understanding that loving our neighbor means sacrificing comfort and peace for the liberation of others.

In my tradition, we often dismiss congregations from worship with a passage from the book of Numbers: "The Lord bless you and keep you; the Lord make his face to shine upon you, and be gracious to you; the Lord lift up his countenance upon you, and give you peace."[1] This, as many of us may already know, is called a "benediction." It comes from the Latin phrase meaning "good word" and the message is meant to accompany you out the door and into the world. While the passage from Numbers is a traditional version, there are as many ways to send people off as there are preachers and pastors to do it. Years ago, I came across one in particular while reading, given by Bishop Woodie White at the 1996 General Conference of the United Methodist Church, which captures the word I'd like to send my readers off with as well:

> And now, may the Lord torment you. May the Lord keep before you the faces of the hungry, the lonely, the rejected, and the despised. May the Lord afflict you with pain for the hurt, the wounded, the oppressed, the abused, the victims of violence. May God grace you with a burning thirst for justice and righteousness. May the Lord give you courage and strength and compassion to make ours a better world, to make your community a better community, to make your church a better church. And may you do your best to make it so, and after you have done your best, may the Lord grant you peace.[2]

---

1. Num 6:24–26.
2. Mountain, "United Women in Faith."

Bibliography

Alexander, Michelle. *The New Jim Crow: Mass Incarceration in an Era of Colorblindness*. New York: New Press, 2011.

———. "When the Spirit Says Go." *Sojourners*, Mar. 2012. https://sojo.net/magazine/march-2012/when-spirit-says-go.

American Civil Liberties Union. "Race and Criminal Justice." https://www.aclu.org/issues/racial-justice/race-and-criminal-justice.

Aptheker, Bettina. *The Dawn Breaks: The Trial of Angela Davis*. Ithaca, NY: Cornell University Press, 1999.

Asch, Chris Myers. *The Senator and the Sharecropper: The Freedom Struggles of James O. Eastland and Fannie Lou Hamer*. New York: New Press, 2008.

Baldwin, James. *The Amen Corner*. New York: Dial, 1968.

———. "Everybody's Protest Novel." In *The Price of the Ticket: Collected Nonfiction 1948–1985*, 38–45. New York: St. Martin's, 1985.

———. *The Fire Next Time*. New York: Vintage, 1993.

———. "The Meaning of the Birmingham Tragedy, 1963." *Our Protestant Heritage: Protestant Council of the City of New York, Panel Discussion*. Recorded Sept. 22, 1963. https://digital.history.pcusa.org/islandora/object/islandora%3A71692?solr_nav%5Bid%5D=768e80f70964edc8e022&solr_nav%5Bpage%5D=0&solr_nav%5Boffset%5D=0.

———. *No Name in the Street*. New York: Dial, 1972.

Barber, William J., II. *Forward Together: A Moral Message for the Nation*. St. Louis: Chalice, 2014.

———. *The Third Reconstruction: How a Moral Movement Is Overcoming the Politics of Division and Fear*. Boston: Beacon, 2016.

———. *We Are Called to Be a Movement*. New York: Workman, 2020.

Black, Edwin. *War against the Weak: Eugenics and America's Campaign to Create a Master Race*. Washington, DC: Dialogue, 2012.

Blain, Keisha. "Ida B. Wells Offered the Solution to Police Violence More Than 100 Years Ago." *Washington Post*, July 11, 2017. https://www.washingtonpost.com/news/made-by-history/wp/2017/07/11/ida-b-wells-offered-the-solution-to-police-violence-more-than-100-years-ago/.

Bloom, Joshua, et al. *Freedom! The Story of the Black Panther Party*. Hoboken, NJ: Levine Querido, 2022.

Bibliography

Bradford, Sarah. *Harriet: The Moses of Her People.* New York: Lockwood, 1886.

———. *Scenes in the Life of Harriet Tubman.* Auburn, NY: Moses, 1869.

Breitman, George. "Foreword." In *Malcolm X Speaks: Selected Speeches and Statements,* edited by George Breitman, vii–viii. New York: Grove Weidenfeld, 1990.

Breitman, George, et al. *The Assassination of Malcolm X.* New York: Pathfinder, 1976.

Bridges, Flora Wilson. *Resurrection Song: African-American Spirituality.* Maryknoll, NY: Orbis, 2001.

Burns, Kalee, et al. "Poverty in the United States: 2021." United States Census Bureau. Sept. 13, 2022. https://www.census.gov/library/publications/2022/demo/p60-277.html.

Butler, Judith, and George Yancy. "What's Wrong with 'All Lives Matter'?" *New York Times,* Jan. 12, 2015. https://archive.nytimes.com/opinionator.blogs.nytimes.com/2015/01/12/whats-wrong-with-all-lives-matter/.

Clinton, Catherine. *Harriet Tubman: The Road to Freedom.* New York: Little, Brown, 2004.

Cone, James. *Black Theology and Black Power.* New York: Seabury, 1969.

———. *A Black Theology of Liberation.* Maryknoll, NY: Orbis, 2015.

Dallard, Shyrlee. *Ella Baker: A Leader behind the Scenes.* Englewood Cliffs, NJ: Silver Burdett, 1990.

Davidson, James West. *'They Say': Ida B. Wells and the Reconstruction of Race.* New York: Oxford University Press, 2009.

Davies, Mark. *Malcolm X: Another Side of the Movement.* Englewood Cliffs, NJ: Silver Burdett, 1990.

Davis, Angela. *Angela Davis: An Autobiography.* New York: International, 1988.

———. "Angela Davis on Continuing to Fight for Change: Interview by Lilia Luciano." *CBS Sunday Morning,* May 29, 2022. https://www.youtube.com/watch?v=lwRIJsLBD6o.

———. *Women, Culture, and Politics.* New York: Vintage, 1990.

Davis, Angela, and Tony Platt. "Interview with Angela Davis." *Social Justice* 40:1–2 (2013) 37–53.

Denker, Angela. "Colin Kaepernick and the Powerful, Religious Act of Kneeling." *Washington Post,* Sept. 24, 2017. https://www.washingtonpost.com/news/acts-of-faith/wp/2017/09/24/colin-kaepernick-and-the-powerful-religious-act-of-kneeling/.

DuBois, W. E. B. *John Brown.* New York: Oxford University Press, 2007.

Fanton, Jonathon F., and Richard Warch. *John Brown.* Englewood Cliffs, NJ: Prentice-Hall, 1973.

French, Scot. *The Rebellious Slave: Nat Turner in American Memory.* New York: Houghton Mifflin, 2004.

Garza, Alicia. "2014–2019: Black Lives Matter." In *Four Hundred Souls: A Community History of African America, 1619–2019,* edited by Keisha N. Blain and Ibram X. Kendi, 382–86. New York: One World, 2021.

Bibliography

———. *The Purpose of Power: How We Come Together When We Fall Apart*. New York: One World, 2020.

Grammy Awards. "Kendrick Lamar." https://www.grammy.com/artists/kendrick-lamar/17949.

Greenberg, Kenneth S. "Name, Face, Body." In *Nat Turner: A Slave Rebellion in History and Memory*, edited by Kenneth S. Greenberg, 3–23. New York: Oxford University Press, 2003.

Haas, Jeffrey. *The Assassination of Fred Hampton: How the FBI and the Chicago Police Murdered a Black Panther*. Chicago: Lawrence Hill, 2019.

Haley, Alex, and Malcolm X. *The Autobiography of Malcolm X*. New York: Ballantine, 1992.

Hamer, Fannie Lou. "Sick and Tired of Being Sick and Tired." In *Can I Get a Witness? Prophetic Religious Voices of African American Women, an Anthology*, edited by Marcia Y. Riggs, 170–81. Maryknoll, NY: Orbis, 1997.

Hamilton, Neil A. *Militias in America: A Reference Handbook*. Santa Barbara, CA: ABC-CLIO, 1996.

Hanch, Kate. *Storied Witness: The Theology of Black Woman Preachers in 19th-Century America*. Minneapolis: Fortress, 2022.

Harding, Vincent Gordon. "God's Avenging Scourge: Nat Turner's Rebellion, the Bloodiest in Slave History, Was Driven by His Prophetic Visions." *Christian History*, 1999, 25–28.

Humez, Jean M. *Harriet Tubman: The Life and the Life Stories*. Madison, WI: University of Wisconsin Press, 2003.

Jacobs, Melissa. "Week under Review: Don't Take Kaepernick's Protest as Disrespect for Military." *Sports Illustrated*, Aug. 29, 2016. https://www.si.com/nfl/2016/08/29/colin-kaepernick-national-anthem-protest-49ers.

King, Coretta Scott. *My Life, My Love, My Legacy*. New York: Henry Holt, 2017.

———. *My Life with Martin Luther King, Jr.* New York: Henry Holt, 1993.

King, Martin Luther, Jr. *The Autobiography of Martin Luther King, Jr.* Edited by Clayborne Carson. New York: Warner, 2001.

———. "Letter from a Birmingham Jail." In *A Testament of Hope: The Essential Writings and Speeches of Martin Luther King Jr.*, edited by James M. Washington, 289–302. New York: Harper Collins, 1991.

———. "Pilgrimage to Nonviolence." In *A Testament of Hope: The Essential Writings and Speeches of Martin Luther King Jr.*, edited by James M. Washington, 35–40. New York: Harper Collins, 1991.

———. "The Three Evils of Society." Address delivered at the National Conference on New Politics, Aug. 31, 1967. MLK Global. https://www.scribd.com/doc/134362247/Martin-Luther-King-Jr-The-Three-Evils-of-Society-1967.

Koester, Nancy. *We Will Be Free: The Life and Faith of Sojourner Truth*. Grand Rapids: Eerdmans, 2023.

Lamar, Kendrick. "Alright." Track 7 on *To Pimp a Butterfly*. Aftermath/Interscope Records, Mar. 2015.

Bibliography

———. "Crown." Track 2 on disc 2 of *Mr. Morale and the Big Steppers*. Aftermath/Interscope Records, May 2022.

———. "DNA." Track 2 on *DAMN*. Aftermath/Interscope Records, Apr. 2017.

———. "FEAR." Track 12 on *DAMN*. Aftermath/Interscope Records, Apr. 2017.

———. "How Much a Dollar Cost." Track 11 on *To Pimp a Butterfly*. Aftermath/Interscope Records, Mar. 2015.

———. "HUMBLE." Track 8 on *DAMN*. Aftermath/Interscope Records, Apr. 2017.

———. "I Can't Change the World Until I Change Myself First: Interview by David Greene." NPR, Dec. 29, 2015. https://www.npr.org/2015/12/29/461129966/kendrick-lamar-i-cant-change-the-world-until-i-change-myself-first.

———. "Mother | Sober." Track 8 on disc 2 of *Mr. Morale and the Big Steppers*. Aftermath/Interscope Records, May 2022.

———. "Savior." Track 5 on disc 2 of *Mr. Morale and the Big Steppers*. Aftermath/Interscope Records, May 2022.

———. "Sherane a.k.a. Master Splinter's Daughter." Track 1 on *good kid, m.A.A.d city*. Aftermath/Interscope Records, Jan. 2012.

Lampley, Karl W. *A Theological Account of Nat Turner: Christianity, Violence, and Theology*. New York: Palgrave, 2013.

Larson, Kate Clifford. *Bound for the Promised Land: Harriet Tubman, Portrait of an American Hero*. New York: Ballentine, 2004.

Lewis, Miles Marshall. *Promise That You Will Sing about Me: The Power and Poetry of Kendrick Lamar*. New York: St. Martin's, 2021.

Marable, Manning. *Malcolm X: A Life of Reinvention*. New York: Viking, 2011.

McMurry, Linda O. *To Keep the Waters Troubled: The Life of Ida B. Wells*. New York: Oxford University Press, 1998.

Mills, Kay. *This Little Light of Mine: The Life of Fannie Lou Hamer*. New York: Dutton, 1993.

Mooney, James W., and Thomas R. West, eds. "Ella Baker: Organization without Dictatorship." In *To Redeem a Nation: A History and Anthology of the Civil Rights Movement*, 197–202. St. James, NY: Brandywine, 1993.

Mountain, Amanda. "United Women in Faith Celebrates Consecration and the Office of Deaconess and Home Missioner." *United Women in Faith*, Sept. 23, 2023. https://uwfaith.org/latest-news/2023/a-holy-moment/.

Mueller, Carol. "Ella Baker and the Origins of 'Participatory Democracy.'" In *Women in the Civil Rights Movement: Trailblazers and Torchbearers 1941–1965*, edited by Vicki L. Crawford, et al., 51–70. Indianapolis: Indiana University Press, 1993.

Myers, Walter Dean. *Malcolm X: By Any Means Necessary*. New York: Scholastic, 1993.

National Archives. "Fred Hampton (Aug. 30, 1948–Dec. 4, 1969)." African American Heritage, accessed Aug. 25, 2020. https://www.archives.gov/research/african-americans/individuals/fred-hampton.

Bibliography

Nault, Jean-Charles. *The Noonday Devil: Acedia, the Unnamed Evil of Our Times*, translated by Michael J. Miller. San Francisco: Ignatius, 2013.

Nelson, Truman. *The Old Man: John Brown at Harper's Ferry*. New York: Holt, Reinhard and Winston, 1973.

Newton, Huey P. *Revolutionary Suicide*. New York: Penguin, 2009.

Orwell, George. *Why I Write*. New York: Penguin, 2005.

Payne, Les, and Tamara Payne. *The Dead Are Arising: The Life of Malcolm X*. New York: Liveright, 2020.

Platon, Adelle. "Kendrick Lamar Opens Up about Meeting President Obama: 'No Matter How High Ranking You Get, You're Human.'" *Billboard*, Feb. 2, 2016. https://www.billboard.com/music/features/kendrick-lamar-meeting-president-obama-6866105/.

Poor People's Campaign. "The Poor People's Campaign: A National Call for Moral Revival." https://www.poorpeoplescampaign.org/about/.

Pulitzer Prizes. "DAMN., by Kendrick Lamar." https://www.pulitzer.org/winners/kendrick-lamar.

Quarles, Benjamin. *Blacks on John Brown*. Cambridge, MA: Da Capo, 2001.

Reklis, Kathryn. "Kendrick Lamar, Public Theologian." *Christian Century*, May 23, 2018, 60–61.

Reynolds, David S. *John Brown, Abolitionist: The Man Who Killed Slavery, Sparked the Civil War, and Seeded Civil Rights*. New York: Vintage, 2006.

Riggs, Marcia Y., ed. *Can I Get a Witness? Prophetic Religious Voices of African American Women, an Anthology*. Maryknoll, NY: Orbis, 1997.

Ross, Rosetta E. *Witnessing and Testifying: Black Women, Religion, and Civil Rights*. Minneapolis: Fortress, 2003.

Rubel, David. *Fannie Lou Hamer: From Sharecropping to Politics*. New York: Silver Burdett, 1990.

Shames, Stephen. *The Black Panthers: Photographs*. New York: Aperture Foundation, 2006.

Silkey, Sarah L. *Black Woman Reformer: Ida B. Wells, Lynching, and Transatlantic Activism*. Athens, GA: University of Georgia Press, 2015.

Stauffer, John, and Zoe Trodd. *Meteor of War: The John Brown Story*. Maplecrest, NY: Brandywine, 2004.

Steinbeck, John. "A Primer on the 30's: For Those Who Have Forgotten What It Was Like . . . For Those Too Young to Know . . ." *Esquire*, June 1, 1960, 85–93.

Stern, Alexandra Minna. *Eugenics Nation: Faults and Frontiers of Better Breeding in Modern America*. Oakland, CA: University of California Press, 2016.

Truth, Sojourner. "Letter to the Daily Inter Ocean (Chicago), December 26, 1880." In *Sojourner Truth as Orator: Wit, Story, and Song*, edited by Suzanne Pullon Fitch and Roseann M. Mandziuk, 201–2. Westport, CT: Greenwood, 1997.

———. *Narrative of Sojourner Truth*. New York: Vintage Classics, 1993.

Bibliography

Turner, Nat. *The Confessions of Nat Turner, the Leader of the Late Insurrection in Southampton, Va.* Edited by Thomas R. Gray. Chapel Hill, NC: DocSouth, 2011.

Washington, Margaret. *Sojourner Truth's America*. Chicago: University of Illinois Press, 2009.

Wells-Barnett, Ida B. *Crusade for Justice: The Autobiography of Ida B. Wells.* Edited by Alfreda M. Duster. Chicago: University of Chicago Press, 1970.

———. "Southern Horrors: Lynch Law in All Its Phases." In *Selected Works of Ida B. Wells-Barnett,* edited by Trudier Harris, 11–42. New York: Oxford University Press, 1991.

West, Cornel. *Democracy Matters: Winning the Fight against Imperialism.* New York: Penguin, 2004.

———. *The Ethical Dimensions of Marxist Thought.* New York: Monthly Review, 1991.

———. "Ethics, Historicism, and the Marxist Tradition." PhD diss., Princeton University, 1980. ProQuest. https://www.proquest.com/docview/303076528?pq-origsite=gscholar&fromopenview=true&sourcetype=Dissertations%20&%20Theses.

———. *Prophecy Deliverance! An Afro-American Revolutionary Christianity.* Louisville: John Knox, 2002.

———. "Cornel West on Ferguson: I Went There to Go to Jail; Interview by Hala Gorani." *CNN,* Aug. 12, 2015. https://www.cnn.com/videos/world/2015/08/12/cornel-west-arrested-ferguson-wrn-intv.cnn.

Williams, Jakobi. *From the Bullet to the Ballot: The Illinois Chapter of the Black Panther Party and Racial Coalition Politics in Chicago.* Chapel Hill, NC: University of North Carolina Press, 2013.

Wright, Scott. *Oscar Romero and the Communion of Saints.* Maryknoll, NY: Orbis, 2009.

Wyche, Steve. "Colin Kaepernick Explains Why He Sat for the National Anthem." NFL, Aug. 27, 2016. https://www.nfl.com/news/colin-kaepernick-explains-why-he-sat-during-national-anthem-0ap3000000691077.

X, Malcolm. "At the Aubudon." In *Malcolm X Speaks: Selected Speeches and Statements,* edited by George Breitman, 88–104. New York: Grove Weidenfeld, 1990.